BEYOND THE HALLS

BEYOND THE HALLS

An Insider's Guide to Loving Museums

MACKENZIE FINKLEA

NEW DEGREE PRESS

COPYRIGHT © 2019 MACKENZIE FINKLEA

BEYOND THE HALLS

An Insider's Guide to Loving Museums

ISBN   978-1-64137-349-4 *Paperback*
         978-1-64137-678-5 *Ebook*

Contents

For my parents, who have always seen the value in museums, and my brother, who goes with me to each one.

Chapter I

Take a Whiff

Hey, you. Yeah, you. The one who just pulled this book from the shelf. First, howdy! I'm thrilled to see you holding a real, physical text in your hands. I'm sure you've spent the better portion of the last week on various screens. Take a break, take a load off, and read this book.

I know I'm not alone when I say that I long for the tangible. I love having book in my hands: the smell, the feel, the look. You just took a whiff, didn't you? That smell only gets better with age. I can't help but buy more books whenever I go to the bookstore, even though I haven't finished more than half the books I own. Even in the digital age, thousands of bookstores and libraries across the country are still thriving—which tells me I'm not the only one who still craves the tangible.

A study conducted by Canon USA found that 65 percent of adults prefer the "tactile experience" of reading a book.[1]

Perhaps I am an absolute sucker for vinyl for similar reasons: the way the needle glides over every ridge; the way the crackles add, a personal, unique quality to the music. The vinyl doesn't crack the same every time you play, and no two records are scratched in the same place. Even though vinyl records became an antiquated technology with the advent of compact discs, they are making a comeback. Contemporary artists are releasing new albums and producing them on both digital and vinyl. This tells us something about how humans tend to romanticize a nostalgic past.

Even though you can read this book digitally, there's nothing quite as satisfying as seeing how far you've made it through the book by the placement of your bookmark. Even though you can listen to Queen on Spotify, there's nothing like experiencing the music how it was meant to be listened to on vinyl. Even though you can see hundreds of thousands of images of the *Mona Lisa* online, there's nothing like the real thing.

---

1   Duffer, Ellen. 2019. "Readers Still Prefer Physical Books". *Forbes.Com.*

I've learned about hundreds of famous people, events, and objects in human history; I've seen and read content of the same volume in textbooks. But seeing John Hancock's signature on the *Declaration of Independence*, touching a piece of the moon, gazing up *at The Creation of Adam* in the Sistine Chapel...these are experiences unlike any other.

This book is all out hanging onto the materialism of human culture. In an increasingly digital world, it's important to remember where we've been as we continue moving forward. How do we do that best? With museums.

You don't have to be a museum lover like me. In fact, maybe it's better if you're not. I don't need to preach to the choir if you're already on the bandwagon, to mix a metaphor. But if you think museums are boring, dusty, and not worthwhile, allow me to show you a new perspective.

Chapter II

Introduction

I love museums: natural history museums, historical homes, art museums, themed environments, libraries... for as long as I can remember, I've enjoyed museums.

Growing up, my favorite museum of all was the Houston Museum of Natural Science (HMNS). Houston, Texas, is known for its first-class museum district and was the backdrop to many of my childhood museum adventures. To this day, the HMNS is my all-time favorite museum, and I've seen a lot of museums.

Even in high school, I would take dates to the HMNS.

Don't knock it until you try it!

I've learned that museums are a really great place to get to know someone.

Plus, it's also been a great way to weed out dates who don't love museums nearly enough...did I mention I've been to a lot of museums?

***

The first public museums appeared in the late seventeenth century, and for the nearly four hundred years since, they have multiplied across the world and become essential means of cultural preservation for all walks of human life. There are an estimated 55,000 museums in the world.[2] In 2016, museums contributed more than fifty billion dollars to the United States economy.[3] Museums are responsible for hundreds of annual research projects that can lead to revelations about the past and innovations for the future.

Lately, though, museums have gotten a bad rap. Approximately 30 percent of the US market has no interest in visiting cultural institutions. People don't visit museums primarily because they would rather be doing something else.[4]

---

2   *Museums of The World 2017.* 2017. 24th ed. Berlin: De Gruyter Saur.

3   *Museums as Economic Engines: A National Study,* commissioned by the American Alliance of Museums and conducted by Oxford Economics, 2017.

4   Dilenschneider, Colleen. 2019. "Admission Fees Aren't What Keep Millennials From Visiting Cultural Organizations (DATA) - Colleen Dilenschneider". *Colleen Dilenschneider.*

In my investigation of this distaste for museums, I've found that museums need to change the way things have always been done. Many museums are behind the times: unchanging, monolingual, and unwelcoming. Some, however, make the effort to change. They are implementing new technologies, becoming more accessible, and diversifying their boards and collections.

If museums are to survive—continue stimulating the global economy, making groundbreaking discoveries, and preserving human culture—they must change. In the meantime, we have many ways to enjoy the ride during this dynamic era of museum evolution.

What's the secret to liking—nay—loving museums? That's where I come in.

***

Without knowing it, I've been preparing for this book my entire life. Every museum, every experience, has led me to the moment I write these words for you!

Welcome to a guidebook for museums by a museum enthusiast. I've formally studied cultural anthropology and human heritage for the last four years, and carefully observed human culture for most of my life.

If you already love museums, welcome to the club! If you want to join the club, you'll surely be ready for initiation by the end of this book. If you hate museums, I hope you'll walk away with a changed perspective by the final chapter.

I believe museums are and should be for everyone—so why would this book be any different? In this book you'll find a little something for everybody: the novice, the historian, the curator, the skeptic, the businessman, and the activist. You'll discover the history of how museums began. You'll hear from experts in the field: directors, curators, exhibit designers, museum educators, and more. I'll share numerous tips and tricks to enhance your overall enjoyment of museums. I will share nearly everything you could ever want to know about how to experience museums—except how to pack the perfect day bag. I'll tell you plenty of personal anecdotes along the way. You will get to know me and why I think museums are endlessly fascinating, totally fun, and—not to mention—incredibly valuable to humanity.

In the many interviews I conducted with current museum professionals, one comment in particular stuck out:

"Museums aren't important. In fact, they're non-essential."

I promise this was not said by a museum professional. In an interview with Joan Marshall, director of the Bryan Museum in Galveston, Texas, she told me someone once said this to her.

Many people believe museums are obsolete because of the internet, but museums are so critical to the preservation of human culture. Museums preserve global and human history in a concrete way; they house the real thing.

***

I hope you find something in this book with which you can connect. If you've ever thought you would rather watch grass grow than visit a museum, you probably just haven't come across a museum with which you can connect. So many people love and have fond memories of museums, and these memories keep them alive. However, many people also find museums boring and outdated—and avoid them at all costs. For museums to continue to exist and chronicle human history for generations, we need to reimagine how we perceive and experience them. Museums, for their part, are already doing much to adapt to the digital age and new generations.

Generation Z tends to value experiences over things. My brother and I are both from Generation Z, and we lost our childhood home and many of our belongings to a hurricane in 2017. Interestingly enough, we didn't become hoarders because of it. If anything, we find it easier to discard things unless they hold significance— or, as Marie Kondo puts it, "spark joy."[5] The things we cherish—such as mementos from various trips—remind us of experiences we value. This may be a product of our upbringing, but studies show Generation Z, overall, spends more disposable income on experiences—like travel and entertainment—than on personal items.[6]

Members of Generation Z, and even millennials, prefer experiences to things—but currently museums are not perceived as experiential. A museum, however, is indeed a collection of experiences. The exhibits have contexts and experiences attached to them, visitors of the museums bring their own experiences, and there are even collective identities portrayed in the halls and

---

5   Kondō, Marie. *Spark Joy: An Illustrated Master Class on the Art of Organizing and Tidying Up*. Ten Speed Press, 2016.

6   Gao, Rebecca. 2018. "We Asked Gen Z About Their Spending Habits". Vice.

archways of each museum. Every piece in a museum has a story: how it was used in the past, how it was found, and how it shifts our previous understanding. A museum is not a collection of stuff, but rather a unique place that can be experienced in dozens of different ways. Let's look to the museum as an experience: a place to change your mind, to further your education, to meet your soulmate, to bond with your loved ones and little ones. A museum is a place where you walk away from your experience changed.

***

Time and time again, museums have changed my life: first dates, school visits, family vacations, and studies both locally and abroad. I have spent the last four years studying human culture, but if we're being honest, I've been preparing for this book my entire life. I've traveled to countless cities, visited hundreds of museums—no joke—and experienced them with others along the way. I've also researched, interviewed, and learned from dozens of other historians, museum professionals, and experts in human culture. This book examines many perspectives.

Part of me has always wanted to write a book. I remember writing a book in my diary in middle school—I think titled something like *Boys, Am I Right?* Though I am still just as perplexed by the actions of the opposite gender, I seemed destined to be an anthropologist from that moment. I wanted to understand people, their actions, and the reasons for their behavior. I was compelled to write this book because I am passionate about museums—borderline obsessed, in fact—and I write often, especially about human culture. I want to share my passion for museums with others and hopefully encourage them to love museums almost as much as I do.

This book is important to me because I've never written something of this length before. Moreover, I've set out to write this book purely because I want to—no one assigned this to me, no one paid me, and no one asked me to do this research. I've put much time, travel, and energy into this book, and it will be a tangible thing to be shared with the world.

You will love this book if you are a museum professional, a museum enthusiast, or fascinated by how humans display their culture and values. You will love this book most of all if you are my parents, brother, or a close friend.

The world is missing a book about museums for people who do not belong to the industry. My hope for this book is that any museum—big or small, historical or scientific—would want to place it in the gift shop. This book is also about American culture, and I would love for people in other countries to view this book as a holistic study of museums and how American culture is affected by them.

I am a firm believer that museums should be accessible to all—so why should this book be any different? If you don't have museum experience, don't worry. I'm here to help. My mom said she sometimes dislikes museums because they make her feel stupid. I've found she feels more connected to museums when given context. She wants help to understand things better. I think this book can be that helpful context for museums, in a general sense. Your other best tool in addition to this book is your unique personality and set of experiences. I'm going to teach you how to experience a museum in your own unique way. You'll never feel stupid in one again.

Consider how you've experienced museums so far. Wouldn't you like to experience them differently? If you love them, great, but your view might still be narrow. If you hate them, I hope to adjust your perspective; hopefully you will leave with a newfound appreciation of museums. This book will provide you with new information and experiences with which to begin your next museum adventure. Let's get started.

Part 1

The Novice

Chapter 1

What is a Museum?

"Museum!" I shouted as we walked through downtown Steamboat, Colorado. "Museum!" I said as we whirred past the small town of Clark. "Museum!" I exclaimed as we watched *The Mummy* during our second movie marathon that week. All of these instances occurred during a few short days in Colorado in the winter of 2019.

You know how something seems to be everywhere when it's on your mind? If you're thinking about buying a green Jeep, you see it everywhere. If you're hung up on someone, you see people who resemble them everywhere. For me, museums are that something. I think about them constantly because I'm borderline obsessed. The average person, I know, probably doesn't think about them nearly as much.

You might be surprised to know that museums are a constant part of your everyday life.

Even if you're not thinking about museums, they are all around you, all the time. Museums are on your college campuses, in your hometowns and city halls, and inside your sports stadiums. They are in movies and television shows. Museums appear in films like *A League of Their Own*, *Black Panther*, and *The Mummy*. They're the central setting of films like *Night at the Museum*—obviously—as well as *Ocean's 8* and *National Treasure*. Museums appear in interviews on CBS Sunday Morning, in specials on National Geographic and in hit songs like "High Hopes" by Panic! at the Disco.

So, what is a museum?

Think about that for a moment. What is a museum to you? For me, a museum is an institution where human culture is housed and displayed for public education and enjoyment. According to the International Council of Museums (ICOM),

A museum is a nonprofit, permanent institution in the service of society and its development, open to the public, which acquires, conserves, researches, communicates and exhibits the tangible and intangible heritage of humanity and

its environment for the purposes of education, study and enjoyment.[1]

This particular definition was adopted in 2007. Now—more than a decade later—ICOM has called for a revised definition, because a museum is truly so much more.[1] People have conceived of museums as rooms full of stuff, but they have so much more to offer.

Museums are places of community.
The George Washington Carver Museum in Austin, Texas, functions as both a collection of cultural materials reflecting the experiences of persons of African descent and also serves as a community center for families in East Austin. The Carver has a library where people can investigate their genealogy, a theater that regularly hosts performances reflecting the African experience, and an art show to which anyone can submit original work. This kind of engaging programming serves hundreds of communities at museums across the country.

---

[1]   "Museum Definition - ICOM". 2019. *ICOM*.

Museums are places for education and learning.
Title I offers federal funds to schools that largely support low-income children and often lack the necessary funding to bring their students to museums. The Dallas Contemporary in Dallas, Texas, provides funding directly to schools to ensure students enjoy field trips to the museum and can access educational programs and materials. Researchers at *Education Next* found that field trips to museums create students who "possess more knowledge about art, have stronger critical-thinking skills, exhibit increased historical empathy, display higher levels of tolerance, and have a greater taste for consuming art and culture."[2] Museums are critical for solidifying ideas and concepts that children learn in the classroom. School field trips to such institutions cultivate well-rounded, productive members of society.

It's not often that 98 percent of Americans agree on anything, but 98 percent of Americans consider museums to be educational.[3]

2   Ryan, Julia. 2013. "Study: Students Really Do Learn Stuff on Field Trips". The Atlantic.

3   *Museums and Public Opinion: Summary of Findings from National Public Opinion Polling,* commissioned by the American Alliance of Museums and conducted by Wilkening Consulting, 2018.

**Museums are places where discovery
and innovation occur.**

Often, museums only exhibit a small fraction of their collection on any given day. Pieces that are not on display are stowed in secure, temperature-controlled vaults, but objects don't just sit in storage collecting dust. Researchers across the world work with these stored items; they investigate painters; the posture of the first humans; and the preservation of artifacts, objects, specimens, and species—to name a few.

Museums are also home to some of the most innovative modes of display: virtual and augmented reality, interactive touch-screens, and even holograms. Exhibit designers constantly update permanent exhibitions. Outside of the public eye, conservators are also some of the forefront innovators of historical preservation methods.

**Museums preserve culture and
catalogue human history.**

I can't help but think of that person who said, "Museums are not important. If the world were ending, we wouldn't need museums." I will concede that—if the world were ending, we would not need museums. We would really need several million escape pods to the moon. For smaller instances of destruction, however, museums can protect a wealth of information.

To understand the importance of preserving the written record, I will share the story about a failure to do just that. The Library of Alexandria, established in Egypt over two thousand years ago, was the pinnacle of research and learning. The library housed thousands of papyri scrolls about mathematics, geography, art, and science. During the Roman Empire, the library slowly deteriorated; later, a large portion of it was destroyed in 48 BCE.[4] The total loss of so many ideas and innovations caused a huge setback for the human race. For an idea of the scope of the damage, imagine one of today's research libraries wholly consumed in a fire. Unfortunately, we don't have to imagine such a catastrophic loss, though. The fire at the National Museum of Brazil in September 2018 nearly destroyed the entire collection and over 200 years of research.

Why bother preserving history, then? What's the practical use? History is preserved for the advancement and betterment of society. No one person can know or

---

4   Chesser, Preston. 2019. "The Burning of The Library Of Alexandria | Ehistory". *Ehistory.Osu.Edu.*

remember everything, so we write things down and preserve them. If we fail to preserve artifacts, we could miss out on world-changing scientific discoveries, innovations, and advancements.

Museums are doing more than we could ever have imagined.

Museums are creating immersive experiences—Museum of Ice Cream in San Francisco, California, and the MICRO Museums in Brooklyn, New York, are two examples. The Museum of Modern Art in New York and the Museum of Fine Arts in Houston are showcasing art exhibits that invite physical interaction. Museums of science and natural history are implementing new technologies that radically alter our experience of science. Gone are the days of cases upon cases and rows upon rows of objects, all collecting dust. Today, we welcome a new era where we experience museums in a revolutionary way.

Forget the boring, dusty museums you thought you knew—get ready to embark on an adventure through the past, present, and future of museums.

Chapter 2

Now What?

"Don't go to a museum with a destination. Museums are wormholes to other worlds. They are ecstasy machines. Follow your eyes to wherever they lead you...and the world should begin to change for you."

—JERRY SALTZ, AMERICAN ART CRITIC

Everyone experiences museums differently. Everyone brings with them individual experiences that shape their interactions with the exhibitions. While there is no right way to experience a museum, there are definitely ways to get the most out of your visit.

What are they? I'm glad you asked.

Option 1: Look before you go.
Museums publish information about their collections, mission, and more across various media. Today, you

merely have to type your query into a search engine, and *voila!* A list of museums and links to their website will appear. Various travel platforms also include thousands of individual reviews of museums.

Museums across the globe have carefully curated websites to help you plan your visit, purchase tickets, and even experience online exhibitions. You can see plenty from the comfort of your own home.

You can even go one step further and research specifics about the museum's offerings. If you were to see an exhibition on Vincent Van Gogh, for instance, you might research the artist himself, the geography of France, or even treatments for depression and mental illness in the nineteenth century.

All of these things arm you with context for your next adventure.

Alternatively, you could do none of this. Sometimes knowing nothing about a museum can make for a very enjoyable experience. An exhibit that is understandable without prior knowledge or context is the mark of successful exhibit.

Option 2: Actually going.

Sometimes, going to the museum in person is not an option due to geographic, monetary, or physical restraints. Fortunately, museum material is incredibly easy to experience and engage with online but—unfortunately—cannot replicate in-person experience.

If you can find the means to go, make it happen.

The in-person experience of seeing the splendor of human creativity at work—from the architecture of the museum down to the tiniest of objects—is unrivaled. You might be thinking you've seen the *Mona Lisa* printed in books and posted online plenty of times, so you don't really need to fly all the way to France.

On the contrary! I thought the same thing, but then I saw the painting in person. The *Mona Lisa*—up close and personal. I get chills just thinking about it. The experience of seeing the fine brushwork, the aging canvas, and the throngs of people waiting their turn is impossible to replicate.

Say you've decided to visit one of the thousands of brick-and-mortar museums on the planet. Congratulations! Keys, wallet, phone...all set to go to the museum. Perhaps you read about it online, and know exactly which exhibitions you want to see. Perhaps you did extra research about noteworthy artists of the twentieth century. Perhaps you didn't, since you enjoy surprise and spontaneity. Either way, there's no right answer. You're here, so what's next?

Option 3: Participant observation.
Participant observation is an ethnographic method you don't need a PhD to use. Participant observation happens when ethnographers, or cultural observers, actively involve themselves in cultural activities in order to gain a better understanding of a cultural group. The observer becomes a participant; participation becomes a method of observation.

They say the best way to learn is by doing, right?

This method ensures you will get more out of a museum experience by interacting with the exhibition, wandering around, reading labels, and experimenting with interactive displays. You could just walk through a museum—breeze through an exhibit—but you have the option to engage with the material. Each individual will engage differently based on his or her experiences. Each individual walks into a museum with his or her own unique perspective; this shapes how individuals process information and even maneuver the exhibition.

And the most beautiful thing? There's no right way.

Exhibit designers imagine someone moving through an exhibition and design an exhibit with this in mind. They attempt to subtly influence the way you move through the space, but this experience is different for every person, every time. Each time you glance over the same material, you'll see things you didn't notice before—that's why museum memberships are wonderfully useful. They offer the opportunity to visit time and time again with incredible ease.

Option 4: Ask for more.

You can also always request more information. The museum might have pamphlets, and there might be museum staff wandering around. Talking with others is among the best—and most memorable—ways to learn about an exhibit. You can even bring a friend to the museum! Their unique perspective will also enhance the exhibition.

Remember when you had the option to investigate the museum before attending? That option exists for you afterward, too. Rather than letting your visit be the conclusion of your experience, you can explore many avenues beyond the halls of the museum itself.

There's always someone or something who knows more.

They can't fit everything into the exhibit!

Option 5: Reflect.
Reflect by yourself or with a friend. I do this a lot after touring a museum. You probably do too, whether you know it or not.

Every museum experience adds to your unique set of life experiences—for better or for worse.

Ask yourself: how did this museum impact me? Why? What was my favorite part? Why? Did I enjoy it? Why? How will this change my thinking in the future? Was there something I learned or saw that I want to share with a friend? Why?

I know I probably sound like an inquisitive three-year-old: why, why, why? But investigating the layers within your thoughts is key to self-reflection. Don't simply ask what you liked. Why did you like something? Questions like these invite you to learn something new about yourself.

***

Of course, you could completely disregard everything I've said. But I think if you even consider these options, you'll find you have a richer museum experience—perhaps a deeper one than you even thought possible.

Just as with anything else in life, you get out of museums what you put into museums. If you act intentionally, not mindlessly, you have everything to gain and achieve. At each museum visit, you are presented with several opportunities; only you can choose if you will take advantage of them.

Chapter 3

Couch to Louvre

Travel is taxing. If I've learned anything from traveling to the world's top museums, it's that travel is costly and exhausting. I find myself on the road or the plane time and again, however, because travel is also amazing. There are little moments—between hours of luggage-lugging and swollen feet—that make it all worthwhile and give you nuggets of memories that stick with you for the rest of your life. Take a moment to reflect—I know you've already been thinking of a few.

When I visited Chicago for the first time, I was in a museum every single day of the trip. Chicago is home to the fifty-seven acre Museum Campus—among the largest plots of land dedicated entirely to museums, even bigger than Museum Island in Berlin.[1] Museum Campus hosts three of Chicago's major museums, and it doesn't even include the Art Institute of Chicago—one of the

---

1   "Chicago Museum Campus | Enjoy Illinois". 2019. *Enjoy Illinois.*

oldest and largest museums in the United States. I had a lot of ground to cover in a very short time.

Chicago's Field Museum is one of the three major natural history museums in the United States, alongside the American Museum of Natural History in New York, NY, and the Smithsonian National Museum of Natural History in Washington, DC. The Field Museum was the last of these three museums for me to check off my bucket list. I took my best friend along, we waited outside for the museum to open, and after two and a half hours inside, we were spent—and we hadn't even seen the whole thing.

We weren't bored. Our bodies had enough.

If you find yourself physically exhausted after an hour or two in the museum, don't feel bad. The two of us couldn't take it, either. I've been asked before about what I call museum stamina—how to see more of the museum without getting tired. Just like training to run a 5K, there are ways to hone your museum stamina—whatever that means for you.

Consider what a successful museum trip looks like for you: having learned something new? Seen something famous? For you, is museum stamina about longer attention span? Is it about seeing as much as possible?

No judgment here. I've spent everywhere from four minutes to four hours in a museum.

Allot time.
On a brief vacation to major cities like Chicago, visitors do not always have the luxury of returning again soon. How can you optimize the visit?

Seeing museums while on vacation can be overwhelming—especially if you are under a time constraint. Time willing, I would sit in the cafe at the Field Museum, take a break, then finish the rest of the museum—I'd probably spend the whole day there. But budgeting your time is a matter of prioritization. I could spend the whole day at the Field Museum, but I would miss lunch with friends, a cruise down the Chicago River, and the stunning views from Willis Tower.

The answer is simple: do what you want. Plan to see what you want, and budget your time as you please.

If you're traveling in a group, this may involve compromise, but you are ultimately in control of your own time budget.

Customize the experience.

In the previous chapter, I discussed five ways to enhance your museum experience. Customizing your experience of the museum is key to your enjoyment. Don't feel obligated to spend time with something because it's famous or reputed; spend time with the objects that move you. Don't feel obligated to spend a certain amount of time in a museum, either. If you aren't feeling a connection with the exhibits, move on—or maybe try one of the exercises in the previous section.

Spend as little—or as much—time as you'd like. When my brother and I visited London, we had already seen two museums in a day, and then found ourselves in Trafalgar Square fifteen minutes before the National Gallery closed. We bolted up the steps to the museum and through what felt like two-hundred rooms to Van Gogh's paintings. I love impressionism and post-impressionist art, so once we found Sunflowers, we remained in that one room until the ushers closed up for the day.

The Dallas Museum of Art (DMA) advocates for a "less is more" model. In their family guide they suggest making your visit "child-size" and focusing on "just a few works of art that spark your child's curiosity." Reminding visitors that general admission to the DMA is free, and "you can return again and again"—if you have that luxury.[2]

Many of the museums in London offer free admission, which helped us feel freer with our time. However, the majority of American museums do not benefit from the same funding European museums enjoy. I often feel guilty if I do not spend my money's worth of time in a museum where admission is over twenty dollars. For a family of four, the cost is even greater. For upwards of one-hundred dollars, a visitor will expect to see a lot and learn a lot.

If you are worried about cost, museums offer admission discounts for certain groups, including youth, students, seniors, veterans, those on government aid, and museum professionals. It also might be worthwhile to invest in a membership; often initial admission cost is deducted from the price of a membership.

---

2   "Family Guide". 2019. Dallas. Dallas Museum of Art. Dallas Museum of Art.

However, guilt doesn't prevent me from spending the money on a museum ticket. I love going to museums.

A national Awareness, Attitudes, and Usage Study (AAU) showed that cost is not the primary reason for low attendance at cultural institutions. Responders simply preferred an alternative leisure activity—in other words, they prefer to be doing something else.[3] Feeling unconnected with what you're seeing is common and completely fine; you have every right to be selective in what you spend time observing.

More on how your museum can work to attract non-visitors in "Relevance, Inclusivity, and Modernity."

When my best friend and I visited the Field Museum, we were not selective; we tried to see the entire thing in less than three hours. For institutions like the Field, the Met, and the Louvre, three hours is not sufficient to spend quality time with a collection. I hesitate to call it impossible, but you might need roller-skates.

Customize your experience. Visit the things you want to see and spend time with the things that fascinate

---

3   Dilenschneider, Colleen. 2019. "Inactive Visitors Are Interested in Attending Cultural Organizations. Why Don't They? (DATA) - Colleen Dilenschneider". *Colleen Dilenschneider.*

you. More joy will bring you more stamina. Don't feel obligated to spend time with something that doesn't inspire you. Your time is precious.

Research.

Let's say you're on a vacation in a city, and getting a membership seems foolish. What then?

The best advice I can offer is to plan.

Ahead of time, consider what you hope to experience. Many museums offer online maps and highlight their most popular artifacts and objects. Developing a plan is especially important for large museums like the Metropolitan Museum of Art and the Louvre.

Think about how you want to experience the day. For me, a museum experience looks like comfy shoes, a fully charged camera, and a granola bar in my purse.

Remember, being spontaneous with your visit is still an option—if you have the time to spare.

For more museum options, check out the previous chapter.

Doing a little research never hurts. That pile of untouched travel books on the shelf can actually be useful.

In the summer of 2019, I was thumbing through several of the travel books my dad purchased to prepare for our trip to Barcelona. I knew I had to find time to visit Park Güell. While not a museum with walls, Park Güell is a UNESCO World Heritage Site. It was originally designed by renowned Spanish architect Antoni Gaudi, and attracts over nine-million people per year.[4]

I expected Park Güell to be crowded; Spain was also experiencing a heatwave at the time. How are we going to do this and enjoy it? The secret was hidden in the travel book. The park is free for entry before its formal opening at eight in the morning. The ground was not yet scalding, and the tourists were only just beginning to arrive.

If you shy away from large crowds, like I do, you don't have to buy a book you'll probably never open. Travel bloggers have saved me many times: do a quick online search to find the best times of year, week, and even day

---

4   "Park Güell - Regulation Conditions for Group Access | April 2013". 2019. Barcelona: Barcelona de Serveis Municipals.

to go to avoid crowds. A little research can go a long way to make for the ideal museum day.

Stretch.

I am completely serious.

Just like training for a 5K, there are ways you can train your body to take on a museum and enjoy yourself to boot.

Think about what you need before you start a workout: a little snack, plenty of water, and a few good stretches. All these things are essential for a museum visit as well.

We tend to push ourselves to the limit on museum visits. We don't drink enough water and we put off meals. I'm definitely guilty of these things. We tend to underestimate the exertion of being on your feet all day.

Museum visits are taxing on the body: standing around in galleries starts to wear down your stamina and enthusiasm faster than walking. Don Glass, host of the Moment of Science podcast, playfully and aptly calls this "gallery feet." When you walk around on any given day, your feet never touch the ground at the same time—each foot actually gets a short rest before stepping again. But when you stand in a museum, both feet are pushing on the ground with no moments for rest. When you stand on both feet, blood pools and fails to circulate as well as it does when walking—so things might get a little uncomfortable.[5]

Breaking up time spent standing helps alleviate gallery feet. Museums often have cafes on site for this exact purpose. Hungry and tired but not ready to leave? Have a snack, take a break, and get back to it.

* * *

The Louvre is the largest museum in the world at 652,300 square-feet.[6]

With more than 35,000 artifacts on display at a time, if you spent just sixty seconds with each object during museum hours—it would take 64 days to see everything.

That's over two months of going to the Louvre every single day—except on Tuesdays, when the museum is closed to the public. Not to mention, it would also cost you over one thousand dollars without a membership.

---

5   "Gallery Feet". 2007. Podcast. *Moment of Science.*
6   Contributor, Jessie. 2018. "The Louvre Museum: Facts, Paintings & Tickets". *Livescience.Com.*

Even if you visited 64 days in a row, artifacts will change and there will be news ones to see, so perhaps "seeing everything" cannot even be done. The Louvre is among the hundreds of museums with thousands of objects on display and thousands more in storage, so the objects continually change. There's always something new to enjoy.

Optimal museum stamina is a balance of attention span and physical endurance.

I'm not here to pressure you in to spending more time in a museum. I'm encouraging you, instead, to spend as little—or as much—time as you like. Above all, allow yourself to be selective.

And it is certainly beneficial to visit more than once.

Museums are a place for sanctuary, not for societal pressure. Museums that pressure are a thing of the past. Museums today are meant to be safe spaces, so let the museum be that for you. Be comfortable with your choices and experience.

Chapter 4

"You Can't Do That!"

"Shan't you and I have fun with my museum?"

—ISABELLA STEWART GARDNER, COLLECTOR
AND MUSEUM FOUNDER

One drizzly, humid morning, I took myself on a date to the Museum of Fine Arts in Houston.

Since I was there particularly early for a weekday, I had the unique honor of having many of the galleries all to myself—well, almost.

Everywhere I went, there was at least one gallery attendant.

Watching me.

Quietly.

From a distance.

I remember wishing they weren't there. I wasn't planning anything chaotic or deviant—I just wanted to enjoy a rare moment of solitude in the gallery.

Once, on a visit to Chicago's Museum of Contemporary Art, I was quietly sketching on a bench in the gallery when an attendant approached me.

"Ma'am, you can't use a pen. I'm going to have to ask you to check your pen at the front desk."

Check my—what?

I can understand why the guards are always watching—I once witnessed an unsupervised child palm a painting. If you're in the museum industry, you know the struggle of people touching everything—even if there is a sign.

I promise I would never touch the art—no matter how bad I want to. The gallery attendants, however, don't know that.

Fair.

I was always taught not to run, not to shout, not to take pictures and never to touch the art. Historian Tony Bennett explains this sort of ingrained behavior learned from museum visits; he calls it the exhibitionary complex.[1] When you walk into a museum, you might see a sign: no flash photography, no touching the art, no food or drink in the gallery, no shouting, no laughing, no breathing—you get the picture.

Rules at the Contemporary Austin

1   Bennett, Tony. "The Exhibitionary Complex." In *Representing the Nation: A Reader*, edited by David Boswell and Jessica Evans, 333-358. London and New York: Routledge, 1999.

Most people see these rules and obey them. They come, they look, they leave. But they seem to leave with a little bit of brainwashing. Bennett's theory states that museums subtly control the behavior of visitors—making for civilized civilians beyond the halls. A visitor learns to be quiet, reserved, and contemplative in a gallery, and takes that with them to the streets, workplace, and home. Bennett claims we are subtly controlled by museums; for decades, we've lived by these rules and assume them as the baseline for most museums.

Until now.

Art, history, and science museums are all morphing into interactive places of wonder and inspiration.

Exhibit designers and curators are turning Bennett's theory on its head. Museums are moving away from static rows of cases to incorporate interactive, tactile exhibits that leave lasting impressions of enjoyment, as well as drive home concepts and ideas.

Museum professionals know you want to touch everything, and they are working to redirect that energy away from fragile objects.

This effort is most evident in science and natural history museums. For decades now, science museums have paved the way for interactive innovations—from simple object panels to human-sized hamster wheels.

History museums are not far behind. They feature actors dressed in period clothing, as well as do-it-yourself lessons in looming and butter churning at museums like the Minnesota History Center.

Art museums, too—despite their long history of being cold and uninviting—are developing immersive art displays, such as the recent exhibition on Van Gogh at the Museum of Fine Arts in Houston. Sculpture exhibits, too, are becoming playgrounds for children and adults of all ages—such as the one at the City Museum in St. Louis, Missouri.

Museums are part of the tourism industry. They compete for the attention of the public against other places where people can choose to spend their time on vacation, like Disneyland. The resulting Disneyfication of museums—turning them into virtual play palaces—is not a negative one.

The common worry is that new entertainment components distract from the content of the museums—but if anything, they make concepts more memorable.

At Space Center Houston, a portion of their permanent displays seeks to explain the difference between mass and weight.

Visitors can step on a scale that shows their weight on earth, and then their weight on other planets, on the moon, in outer space, and even in the sun. This simple and, truthfully, comical display effectively demonstrates the relationship between mass and weight.

Museums are, now more than ever, places of entertainment as well as learning.

Bennett's exhibitionary complex, however, is still alive and well. While American museums are pushing to innovate and entertain, European museums—like the British Museum and the Louvre—remain largely unchanged. They are still, however, remarkable in their own respects.

Even if a museum is not implementing new technologies, you can still do a lot more than stand there and observe the artifacts. You can break free from the exhibitionary complex. Of course, you should honor the rules of the museum—but you don't have to just stand there! Why would you want to?

My brother once described it as "absolutely mind-numbing to look at a painting or objects and then try to read a tiny plaque with minimal information—dozens or hundreds of times." My brother is not alone in describing this sense of staggering boredom in reaction to a museum.

This same sort of experience inspired Nick Gray to develop a series of museum tours, and later a company, Museum Hack. In Gray's model, guides lead visitors on tours that seek to engage and entertain—loaded with group activities and intriguing back-stories about artifacts.[2]

Museum Hack has developed tour packages for visitors to enjoy and professionals to observe. They offer everything from interactive games to photo challenges—even yoga in the galleries, as well as the chance to enjoy the art while lying on the floor.

---

2   Gray, Nick. "How I learned to stop hating and love museums." Filmed May 2015 in Washington, DC. TED video, 17:30.

Though Gray's interactive tours seem novel, museum educators have been doing this for years—often under the radar of the average visitor. Unless you've booked a tour through a museum before, you might not even know that museum educators exist.

The museum educator's job is to develop and execute programs that help visitors better understand concepts, artifacts, and objects—and these programs can get pretty creative.

Siobhan McCusker is a museum educator at the Blanton Museum of Art in Austin, Texas. She took me on a private tour of the galleries with a few friends. Three of us met McCusker on a busy Thursday afternoon, unsure of what to expect. We met her on the main floor of the museum in the middle of a large atrium and introduced ourselves.

"Lovely to meet you all. I invite you to make yourselves comfortable and find a spot to lay on the floor."

I looked back at her. "What?"

"If you look up, one of the best and most comfortable ways to enjoy this piece is on one's back," she replied matter-of-factly.

Sure enough, there was a massive sculpture droop-
ing from the ceiling just above our heads. My friends
and I looked at each other, looked around the atrium,
and back at one another—still wondering if this was
truly allowed.

We slowly sank to the ground and listened as McCusker
told us about the sculpture. She asked us questions about
how the art made us feel, as well as how we thought the
artist may have felt while creating it. That sculpture is
absolutely unforgettable to me know.

As we rounded the corner of the Art of the Spanish
Americas gallery, McCusker stopped us.

"Okay, I need one of you to close your eyes and another
to safely guide them into the gallery."

We blindly trusted her—literally. One of my friends
closed her eyes and the other lead her into the gallery.
McCusker led us to a large painting at the end of the gallery and invited me to describe the painting in as much
or as little detail as I wished to my blindfolded friend.

As I attempted to describe a rather ornate portrait, I
discovered so many details within the painting. My
communication skills were certainly tested—as was my

friend's imagination. Once the blindfold was removed, she observed the painting was almost nothing like she had pictured it—but that's part of the fun.

I so enjoyed this game that I decided to test it once again...on a friend who hates contemporary art.

Three of us were on a spring break pit-stop to the Museum of Fine Arts in Houston. I told him I would have our other friend, Hannah, close her eyes and I would lead her into the next gallery. Then, he would have to describe the artwork to her.

"You can't do that!" he whispered loudly.

"Who said?"

With an eyebrow raised, he followed me into the next gallery: modern and contemporary art. I stopped them in front of a piece by Joan Miró, *Painting (Circus)*—just abstract enough to be a challenge.

He sighed heavily and began to describe the painting, and we spent the rest of the visit playing this game in each gallery—and many more museums thereafter. When we visited the Institute of Contemporary Art

(ICA) in Boston, we even tried blindly drawing the artwork based on the description that was offered.

I don't want to say that the game totally changed his perspective on contemporary art, but a videography installation[3] from the ICA now ranks among his favorites.

***

During all the times I've played this game, I have never once been stopped by a gallery attendant. My friend's hesitation to participate in the game was a result of the same ingrained thoughts that Bennett discusses in his theory on museums. Though no one explicitly told him so, he felt the museum was a place for restraint—not for fun.

As we are greeted by this new era of participatory museums, we can do so much more than just go, look, and leave. Museums don't have to be—and aren't—boring. It's up to the visitors to push the boundaries and disrupt the status quo.

Just don't touch the art.

---

3   Kjartansson, Ragnar. "The Visitors," Video, 2012.

Part 2

The Historian

Chapter 5

Not So Humble Beginnings

In 1492, Columbus sailed the ocean blue.

Though he certainly was not the first to do so, Spanish explorer Christopher Columbus' voyage to the Americas is among the best-known expeditions in the world. There were a great number of such expeditions across the globe in the sixteenth and seventeenth centuries. On these voyages, explorers did more than just visit. They took a few souvenirs each place they went: some purchased, some traded, and many stolen.

Archaeology, the study of human history through excavations, is a subfield of anthropology, the study of humanity and human cultures. Before the professions of anthropology and archaeology were formalized with rules, regulations, and permits, people in the world lived by the mantra of finders keepers. If they saw something they wanted or thought of value, they took it. Many of the items in the British Museum were acquired in this manner—more on this in "Righting Wrongs." When a large statue of Pharaoh Ramses II was discovered, British diplomat Henry Salt hired circus performer and weightlifter Giovanni Battista Belzoni to help retrieve it—or, rather, to rob a tomb.[1]

During this era of exploration, the wealthy often spent months traveling to various corners of the world, and brought back souvenirs, fossils, bones, and other curiosities—which they then proudly displayed in their parlors upon their return home. Wealthy families would host dinner parties and invite over friends to showcase their private collections and boast of their worldliness.

These vast, private collections of natural and man-made objects were arranged in drawers, placed on shelves, and even mounted on the ceiling. Some collections of curiosities became large enough to fill an entire room.

Often, collections were eventually opened to the public—these became the first museums. Private collections became public institutions, places which everyone could

---

1   Fagan, Brian. 2018. *Little History of Archaeology*. New Haven and London: Yale University Press.

enjoy, where they could grapple with how they fit into this life and the world.

"Given our curious natures and our innate desire to collect, it is no wonder the grand modern museums has its humble roots firmly planted in the privately owned collections of extraordinary objects from the past."

—KATHLEEN HAVENS, DIRECTOR OF
CURRICULUM AND CONTENT AT THE HOUSTON
MUSEUM OF NATURAL SCIENCE

Natural history encompasses everything from geological formations to human culture. Man is a part of nature, and everything from our biology to the societies we create is exhibited and explored in natural history museums.

Conrad Gessner, a sixteenth-century zoologist, may have started the first natural history museum in his home in Zurich.[2]

Some say the Muséum national d'Histore naturelle, established in 1635 in Paris, France, was the first natural history museum. Its origins can be traced back to the seventeenth-century plant collection of King Louis

---

2   Vincent H. Rash, Ring T. Cared. 2003. *Encyclopedia of Insects*. London: Elsevier.

XIII, but it was not institutionalized until 1793, during the French Revolution.[3]

If you ask me, the first natural history museum was the Ashmolean Museum on the campus of Oxford University.

Elias Ashmole donated his cabinet of curiosities to Oxford University in 1677. The Ashmolean—named after the generous donor—was the first natural history collection to open its doors to the public in 1683. In doing so, the Ashmolean Museum "firmly established the official use of the word 'museum.'" It is the oldest university museum in the world.[4]

To me, a museum is for all. By being among the first collections to open to the public, the Ashmolean propelled the museum industry as we know it today. It set a standard of museums as public places for education where people can see unique and historic specimens on view from around the world.

Other types of museums were appearing during this age of enlightenment, as well, so to truly name the first

---

3   "The French National Museum of Natural History." Convention on Biological Diversity. Secretariat of the Convention on Biological Diversity, April 3, 2008.

4   Andi Stein, Beth Bingham Evans. 2009. *An Introduction to the Entertainment Industry*. New York: Peter Lang Publishing.

museum is difficult. However, the institutions that laid the groundwork for museums as we know them today were often these private cabinets of curiosities—later turned into public museums, especially on university campuses. Private collections were donated so researchers and students could access and study specimens, as they still do today.

The World's Fair

During the age of enlightenment, technology was advancing at a rapid pace, and people were traveling far from home with more ease than ever before. World's fairs—beginning in Paris in 1844—became the time and place for nations to join together in one city and showcase their best work in the field of industry. By sharing this wealth of knowledge, miraculous innovations were more rapidly globalized.

Another great benefit of the world's fairs was the iconic structures built to house such expositions; these ultimately became some of the most prominent museums and monuments in the world. Just as cities will often invest in new infrastructure prior to hosting the Olympics, nations would commission elaborate, cutting-edge structures to convey the power of their national industry. The Eiffel Tower is one such example.

The tour Eiffel was only intended to be temporarily on display for twenty years—beginning as the centerpiece for the Exposition Universelle of 1889 in Paris—but it proved to be quite valuable.

We have the 1893 Colombian Exposition to thank for both the Field Museum and the Museum of Science and Industry in Chicago. The Saint Louis Art Museum, the Please Touch Museum in Philadelphia, and the lesser-known Texas Memorial Museum in Austin all run out of buildings erected for World's Fairs.

After the first exposition, world's fairs became a common occurrence in various cities throughout the world—usually to celebrate some historic milestone for the nation. The 1893 Colombian Exposition in Chicago celebrated the four-hundredth anniversary of Columbus' arrival in the Americas. The 1889 Exposition Universelle in Paris celebrated the centennial of the storming of the Bastille. The 1936 Texas Centennial Exposition celebrated the anniversary of independence from Mexico.

Not only are world's fairs incredibly fascinating, but they are also notable because they contributed to the widespread opening of natural history and science museums. There, nations could proudly display innovations and accomplishments year-round—instead of only for the brief duration of the exposition.

Natural (Science) History

In many cases, science and natural history museums are very similar. After all, both attempt to explain the world as it is, has been, and possibly will be through a biological lens. Science museums may largely focus on technology and industry, but you can't have things like lightbulbs, cars, and computers without understanding the natural resources that make them whole and functional.

Few cities have the luxury of having two separate buildings—one for science and one for natural history—like Chicago, which hosts the Museum of Science and Industry and the Field Museum of Natural History. London also has one of the most famous natural history museums, as well as a renowned science museum not too far away.

Alternatively, many cities have combined the two: Houston, Texas, the fourth largest city in the United States, is home to the Houston Museum of Natural Science. This museum has cornered the city market in all things natural history and science and is among the most visited museums in the country.

Though there is much overlap, and many museums combine the two, there is certainly a visible difference between science and natural history museums.

The largest difference is that science museums do not display anthropological collections. Science museums focus, instead, on human and industrial advancement; they focus on how things work and mechanical marvels—from man-made bicycles to metabolic life cycles. They discuss humans and their impact on the planet, but do not delve specifically into various human cultures.

The contents of a natural history museum, in contrast, are fairly systematic. You'll find paleontology, zoology, botany, astronomy, geology, and anthropology. The differences in each of the natural history museums you might encounter are contained in the quality, rarity, and variety of the items—but the categories of exploration are largely the same.

Worlds Collide
Science museums and natural history museums have also been known to collide with art museums.

Though science and art are at odds with one another—competing for academic attention—they work beautifully together in the world of museums.

Science museums without art would be of no visual interest and would lack cohesive explanations for the exhibits.

While I was working at Texas Memorial Museum, there was a temporary exhibit on view: *the Buzzsaw Sharks of Long Ago.* Ray Troll, an artist and fossil enthusiast, worked with scientists at the Idaho Museum of Natural History to develop a traveling exhibition on the prehistoric Helicoprion—an extinct, shark-like fish. With a few fossils and a lot of research, Troll developed utterly wacky paintings, sketches, and prints depicting this long-extinct shark. His artwork helps visitors understand what this prehistoric shark may have looked like from fossils of its teeth and jaw alone.

"What I enjoy most as an exhibit designer and an artist is working with the scientists [...] and collection managers and being a mediator, as an artist between all of these people who

are writing the stories [...] interviewing them about what do they want to say to the public."

—JOHN MAISANO, ARTIST-IN-RESIDENCE AND
EXHIBIT DESIGNER AT THE UNIVERSITY OF
TEXAS AND TEXAS MEMORIAL MUSEUM

Science often needs art to communicate concepts; conversely, art often needs science to be produced and preserved.

Art museums without science would lack deep contextual understanding of creation and preservation methodologies. We weren't around to watch Leonardo Da Vinci paint the *Mona Lisa*, but studies of the painting can help us understand the process of the painter, the age of the painting, and even the composition of the paints themselves.

In the summer of 2018, I wandered down to the Museum of Fine Arts Houston for an exhibition titled *Hidden Layers*. The exhibit showcased European paintings alongside x-ray images of each painting, which conservators captured with x-radiography and infrared reflectography to reveal artists' original sketches beneath layers of paint.[5]

---

5   "Hidden Layers: Painting and Process in Europe, 1500–1800". 2018. Houston: Museum of Fine Arts Houston.

Conservators at the Harvard Art Museums can reference a pigment library of the world's rarest pigments in-house to analyze and restore paintings vital to American heritage.

Art and science always coexist.

In the Morian Hall of Paleontology at the Houston Museum of Natural Science, visitors can watch scientists work on fossils in real time. Similarly, visitors can watch conservators at the Museum of Fine Arts, Boston, do work on paintings and sculptures.

The creativity of exhibit design is itself an art form implemented at museums of art and science alike. Natural history museums, however, currently lead the pack in the implementation of entertaining exhibit designs.

Disneyfication

Today, natural history museums are moving away from static cases of artifacts toward dynamic exhibits that utilize visual and interactive technology. Technology continues to be used to change the way we experience museums, as well as the means by which we learn and absorb information.

We go to museums to learn, and museums are implementing creative exhibition design methods to help make learning fun and information stick. They have slowly upgraded exhibits from static displays to pieces that educate in more engaging ways than text panels.

The Natural History Museum in London is in transition—split between an elaborate technological upgrade and a time-honored tradition. The museum contains an entire hall with cases of rock samples and precious gems, but also features an immersive—and terrifying—exhibit on natural disasters. The exhibit invites you to stand on an earthquake simulator and experience a 6.9 magnitude earthquake.

The California Academy of Sciences saw an opportunity—due to earthquake damage—to completely rebuild their museum. The new Cal Academy is a perfect example of the new, entertainment-driven exhibitions that older museums are beginning to implement. It is truly reminiscent of Disneyland.

The life of a museum starts as one thing and transforms into another by redefining itself. Natural history museums now have to compete with places like Disneyland for crowds and attention. In order to maintain public interest, natural history museums are shifting to new methods of exhibit design that include popular science and a more engaging experience—like one you might have at an amusement park.

Science can be entertaining to the masses in uncomplicated ways.

At the heart of the Houston Museum of Natural Science, there is a Foucault Pendulum—a massive brass bob anchored to the end of a long string, three stories long. Twenty-four hours a day, seven days a week, this pendulum swings back and forth one-hundred-and-eighty degrees—knocking down a string of little wooden dominoes arranged in a circle.

Every Houstonian knows that—if you stand by the pendulum long enough—you will be lucky enough to witness it knock down a domino. A most satisfying feeling.

How can it knock down a ring of blocks if it only pivots one-hundred-and-eighty degrees? The earth's rotation! As the pendulum swings back and forth, the earth spins below it—that's the gist of it, at least.

French physicist Léon Foucault designed this contraption in 1851 to demonstrate the earth's rotation.[6]

This display has been repeated and modified in different ways at museums around the world. The display succeeds because of the attention and fascination of the public—and it's not too hard to build.

***

History is everything that has already happened—right up to the moment you read these words. History, as a whole, is a lot to tackle for one museum, but not to worry—there are hundreds.

While the beginning of museums is rooted in collections of artifacts, there are many varieties of museums—from art museums and niche museums to libraries, archives, and historical homes. Each museum serves a unique purpose and models a different aspect of human history and human understanding.

---

6   Oprea, John. "Geometry and the Foucault Pendulum." *The American Mathematical Monthly*102, no. 6 (1995): 515–22.

Chapter 6

How Does That Make You Feel?

"Art is not always about the pretty things. It's about who we are, what happened to us, and how our lives are affected."

—ELIZABETH BROUN, FORMER DIRECTOR OF THE
SMITHSONIAN AMERICAN ART MUSEUM

I have only been moved to tears by a painting once in my life.

I had made it my mission to see *His Life in Art*—a 2019 exhibit on Van Gogh—while it was on view at the Museum of Fine Arts Houston. Featuring fifty of his master works, this exhibition had been over three years in the making; the last Van Gogh exhibition in Houston, Texas, was nearly seventy years prior.[1] Van Gogh

---

1   Watkins, Katie. "Inside Look: More Than 50 Rarely-Loaned Van Gogh Works On Display at The Museum of Fine Arts, Houston." Houston Public Media, March 18, 2019.

exhibits rarely occur in the United States since the Dutch artist's work is in such high demand.

You've heard of him. Everyone has.

He is a household name and a post-impressionist icon.

You've probably seen *Starry Night*, 1889; it is one of the most recognizable pieces of art in the world.

I set off with a pair of friends to see the exhibition—we began together, then slowly went our separate ways. I followed the massive crowd of people filed around the perimeter wall of the exhibition, patiently waiting my turn to see work after original work by my artistic hero.

When I was in the third grade, I remember being assigned a project on an iconic American artist. We would choose anyone from music, to literature, to art. In my choice to do a project on Van Gogh, I seem to have conveniently left out the 'American' part. I then had to start over with a project on Jackson Pollock.

Can you blame me, though? Van Gogh's work is so impactful and widely known that little eight-year-old me conceived of him as an American icon.

All the paintings were arranged in chronological order to illustrate the artist's emotional and physical turmoil over the course of his prolific, yet brief, ten-year career.

I was about halfway through the exhibition when my eyes landed on this painting.

Head of a Woman by Vincent Van Gogh, 1885.

I cannot explain it.

I didn't understand why an objectively unattractive painting was moving me to tears almost instantly.

The feeling was just so visceral. I looked at that painting, and I felt Van Gogh: his pain and his struggle. I felt the feelings of the subjects in his paintings: tired, weary, and misunderstood. I was just left in awe about what was in front of me as I imagined him creating the painting—brushstroke by brushstroke—a peasant farmer sitting in a chair right in front of him.

Before moving to Paris, Van Gogh painted peasant farm workers from his community in dark, somber colors.

If you haven't had such an intense response to art yet—be it joy, awe, or sadness—then you haven't been to the right art museum yet.

I hear all kinds of responses all the time. "Art museums just aren't my thing." "Art museums are boring." "Art museums are intimidating."

I will admit my heart belongs to natural history museums, but art museums are magical—and they too have played a vital role in the establishment of the museum industry.

Natural history museums are not alone at the forefront of innovative museum design. While many art museums still maintain the traditional, frame-to-frame exhibition model, exhibit designers and curators are also introducing immersive experiences.

The Van Gogh exhibit at the Museum of Fine Arts Houston, existed in two parts: a chronological display of his masterworks, as well as another room brimming with engaging activities and photo opportunities.

While natural history museums were among the first to be formally institutionalized, art museums have existed for just as long—and are continuing to grow and evolve.

Divine Inspiration

Human history shows evidence of artistic ventures—cave paintings—dating as far back as the Neolithic Revolution and the advent of leisure time.

Some fifteen-thousand years later, the birthplace of art museums, as public spaces for viewing works of art, has its roots in religion. Clergy commissioned artists to create murals to honor divine idols—on the walls of cathedrals especially. Some of the oldest paintings on display today are altar pieces from the Middle Ages. The oldest works of art you will find on display are sculptures.

In 1471, Pope Sixtus IV opened his collection of Roman sculpture to the public—making it the oldest public collection of art in the world. The pope's collection was eventually developed into the Capitoline Museums in 1734.[2]

Royalty subsequently commissioned artists to depict them in a god-like fashion for their palaces. Places of worship became some of the first places where art was displayed for the public to enjoy—followed by palaces accessed only by men of wealth and status, like Versailles. Monarchs would host grand dinner parties to showcase their art and collections.

---

2   "The World's Oldest Museums." Museums of the World Museums. Semantika. Accessed November 8, 2019.

Humans have a habit for collecting. The production of art was popularized by the invention and sale of pigments and paints—and in the same fashion as the cabinets of curiosities in the previous chapter, noblemen began collecting works of art. We have their expensive habits to thank for the formation of early art museums.

In 1764, Catherine the Great purchased the art collection of Johann Ernst Gotzkowsky for display and established the second-largest art museum in the world: The State Hermitage Museum in St. Petersburg, Russia.[3]

People collected art for hundreds of years prior to the first art museum, but these collections were limited to elite social circles. These early private collections help to establish notions that continue to prevail today, saying art museums are only for the rich and elite. This statement is fair regarding the first art museums. Versailles sees millions of visitors annually today, but before it became a museum, the palace was only available to those wearing silver shoe buckles.

3   "The Acquisition of J.E. Gotzkowsky's Collection by Catherine II." 1764
     The Acquisition of J.E. Gotzkowsky's Collection by Catherine II. Accessed
     November 8, 2019.

At the end of the eighteenth century, the French royal collection was nationalized, giving us the Louvre: the largest, most visited art museum in the world.[4]

Back across the pond, the Pennsylvania Academy of the Fine Arts opened in 1805 as the first art museum and art school in the United States. There are over seven hundred university art museums in the United States, making it the largest category of art museum in the nation.[5]

University art museums were—and are—a place where students can study the cultures across continents and time. While university art museums were the first public places for art appreciation in the United States, the need for a public educational space remained. This need was especially strong for those who could not afford higher education or weren't allowed to enroll—like women.

Then came the Met.

---

4   Oliver, Bette Wyn. 2007. *From Royal to National: The Louvre Museum and the Bibliothèque Nationale.* Lanham: Lexington Books.

5   The Editors of Encyclopaedia Britannica. "Pennsylvania Academy of the Fine Arts." Encyclopædia Britannica. Encyclopædia Britannica, Inc., September 27, 2006.

"You can walk in the door and literally work through the entire history of human creation, from its earliest forms... through today."

—CARRIE BARRATT, FORMER CURATOR OF AMERICAN ART AT THE METROPOLITAN MUSEUM OF ART[6]

The state of New York decided it was time for a place that was "open and accessible to the public [...] throughout the year," and in 1870 granted articles of incorporation to the Metropolitan Museum of Art "for the purpose of establishing and maintaining [...] a museum and library of art [...] encouraging and developing the study of the fine arts [...] advancing the general knowledge [...] and to that end [...] furnishing popular instruction and recreations."[7]

The Metropolitan Museum of Art first opened its doors in 1872. It is the largest art museum in the United States and the third-most-visited art museum in the world.

The Met is like a fairy-tale. Aside from being a museum-lover's dream, the Met is a magical place that you see and hear people discuss in movies. It also hosts the

---

6   YouTube. "A World of Art: The Metropolitan Museum of Art." Great Museums, December 9, 2009.

7   Disturnell, John. *New York As It Was and As It Is*. New York, NY: D. Van Nostrand, 1876.

Met Gala, one of the largest red-carpet events of the year. This art museum is treasured in the United States and a pillar of our national identity.

The Big Whoop

Allow me to hop off my soapbox to wrap up this little art history lesson.

Art museums are a huge portion of the museum industry, famous and beloved. Art museums do pretty well for themselves. They are, collectively, the most visited type of museum in the world.

But let's talk about the elephant in the room. Why do people visit art museums?

Jess Cotton, contributor to *The Book of Life* online publication by *the School of Life*, contends, "Many of us show up at these [art] museums more out of guilt than genuine pleasure. The prestige of art – as opposed to any spontaneous enthusiasm – is what seems to keep a sizeable share of people coming through the doors." The article suggests we've been utterly convinced that art is important but find it difficult to say why.[8]

8   Cotton, Jess. "What Art Museums Should Be For." The Book of Life. The School of Life, August 24, 2016.

Why are works of art—and therefore art museums—important? I'll offer two reasons.

First, art and art museums catalogue human history.

Art museums are encyclopedias of human creativity, chronicling the evolution of art through time and space. Art is often a product of the time and circumstances in which it was created. Realistic works of art serve as nearly-photographic evidence of the landscape and architecture of the past. Abstract works of art reveal human emotions as a byproduct of the events and lifestyle of the time in which they lived.

Second, art and art museums are therapeutic for the people who observe them.

I asked a friend once if they had a favorite art museum; they responded that art museums just aren't for them. Surely, they aren't the only one who feels this way or the stigma around museums wouldn't exist. People who think they dislike art museums, however, probably just haven't come across art they can connect with. Perhaps that art hasn't yet been created.

Art and art museums are the places most in touch with human emotion. People go to art museums to connect with something, and in that way art museums can be places of healing—bringing us back to art's religious background.

"I was not religious enough as a young person to become a rabbi, but I found solace and challenge in the bigger ideas posed by contemporary art."

—ADAM LERNER, FORMER DIRECTOR OF THE
MUSEUM OF CONTEMPORARY ART DENVER[9]

There's more to art than just the image. Art tries to convey some bigger statement. It's not just a dot on an otherwise blank canvas; it's a personal statement about loneliness. It may not be splattered paint on a wall but rather a metaphor for the scattered mind.

Art is thoughtful and portrays something about reality. Sometimes, you just have to look beyond the surface.

"There's something absolutely thrilling about seeing the work itself."

—EVERETT FAHY, FORMER CURATOR OF EUROPEAN
PAINTINGS AT THE METROPOLITAN MUSEUM OF ART[10]

---

9   Martin, Jeff. "Go Forward Move Ahead". *Museum Confidential*. NPR, September 20, 2019.

10 YouTube. "A World of Art: The Metropolitan Museum of Art." Great Museums, December 9, 2009.

You learn about art in school—the *Mona Lisa*, *American Gothic*, *Starry Night*—but nothing can compare to seeing art in person. An image in a textbook or online cannot compare to getting up close and personal with a painting: looking at the detail, brushstrokes, and woven pieces of the canvas. Observing a painting in person offers insight into how the artist created that painting, which in turn offers insight into the human experience. Then you start to feel something, and that is the big whoop about art museums.

Art museums are about human connection through time and space. Art itself is a time traveler—a message from people long gone. How wonderfully serendipitous to imagine that the art was intended for you to see right in that moment, when you needed it most.

Chapter 7

History of the Everyday

"Real museums are places where time is transformed into space."

—ORHAN PAMUK, RECIPIENT OF THE
NOBEL PRIZE IN LITERATURE

My parents live in a home that is over 130 years old. Built before one of the most devastating storms in US history, the 1900 Galveston hurricane, the house has survived several more hurricanes and housed several generations. On a hot spring day, people line the sidewalk around the block to walk through our family home on the Galveston Historic Homes Tour. For us, the house is quotidian—but for visitors it stands as a monument to the Victorian era and a once-thriving coastal city.

In this chapter, I will introduce you to four scholars on historic houses and historic house museums. Together, we will uncover the dynamic history of memorializing and preserving entire estates.

Historic house museums are far more numerous than any other type of museum.[1] As such, historic house museums are a major component of the museum and tourism industry. Not only are they abundant, but admission is often cheap or free. Exceptions to the rule include prominent historic house museums belonging to people like Elvis Presley or George Washington.

The Purpose

The prominence of historic homes is often determined by their importance to American history or culture. Jillian Barto, digital assets cataloguer at Mount Vernon, states that the significance of a house lies in the "historical event that happened at the site, or the historical person who lived there."[2] Mount Vernon—the home of the first president of the United States—is a prime example. Admission costs twenty dollars and often requires prior planning due to high tourism traffic. But historic

---

1   "Home Page." AASLH. Accessed 2018.
2   Barto, Jillian. "The New House Museum: How the Development of Modern House Museums Are Changing the Philosophies and Standards of Interpretation and Preservation." 2012.

house museums of this cost and reputation are not the majority.

The Elisabet Ney Museum in Austin, Texas, for example, is completely free—and the oldest museum in Texas.

The goal of each historic house museum is to preserve the past without compromising the context of the museum, which gives us insight into its history.

The Challenge

Giovanni Pinna—theoretical museologist and former chairman of the International Committee for Historic House Museums—says historic house museums are unique from other types in that they "are used to conserve, exhibit or reconstruct real atmospheres which are difficult to manipulate if one does not wish to alter the very meaning of 'historic house.'"[3] To rearrange the furniture, redecorate, repaint, or otherwise alter the atmosphere would strip away some of the history.

Pinna also taught me that a key difference exists between historic houses and historic house museums. Historic house museums go beyond the halls and phys-

---

3   Giovanni Pinna. "Introduction to Historic House Museums," Museum International 53 (2001): 4-9.

ical structure and include the original collections and furnishings of the homeowner. A historic house is one thing standing alone, but a historic house museum also offers context.

In other words, the objects make the museum.

In the museum world, objects made by humans are artifacts. Without the artifacts, a historic home retains little to no context.

What is a museum without objects and artifacts? Empty, or worse, a building full of disoriented tourists.

A museum is a building with objects and artifacts, and a historic house museum is a historic building filled with such artifacts. These objects add to the context and history of events that happened there.

Evoking Nostalgia

Nostalgia—a buzzword for the decade. In an era of reboots and sequels, we crave the feeling of nostalgia. Romanticizing the past just feels so good. I love to thumb through old photos, and I'm a big fan of sharing Buzzfeed nostalgia-themed listicles.

Museology professor Mónica Risnicoff de Gorgas advocates for nostalgia and romanticism in the historic house museum. I couldn't resist exploring her perspective.

De Gorgas sees historic house museums as a monument to the past in addition to "a place where people have lived out their life"; sometimes, a house becomes a museum for this very reason.[4] I have a feeling Oprah Winfrey's estate will be an experience comparable to visiting Graceland someday, for instance.

A house is a home—a place where people spend time, create stories, and form memories. De Gorgas believes historic house museums have a "highly evocative power" that creates an "intimate link between collective and personal memory."[5]

The Tenement Museum of New York paints a realistic view of the local immigrant experience through replicas of apartments, actors, and even food tastings. Walking through the Tenement Museum sends you back in time and invites you toward a cultural and temporal experience.

4   De Gorgas, Mónica Risnicoff. "Reality as Illusion, the Historic Houses That Become Museums." *Museum Studies: An Anthology of Contexts*, 2nd ed., Wiley-Blackwell (2012): 324–328.
5   Ibid.

The Tenement Museum, like other house museums, not only memorializes the past, but also evokes strong feelings of nostalgia in its visitors.

Freeze Frame!

The best way for a historic house to evoke nostalgia is by fossilizing the past: taking a moment in the history of the home and freezing it in time. A historic house gives the impression that its owner suddenly departed, or vanished while setting the table for afternoon tea.

The historic home, when left untouched, becomes a time capsule with context about the past. A historic house museum contextualizes a moment in time and space through the placement of objects throughout the home.

A historic house museum can be compared to an archaeological excavation site. Such excavation sites are often located where cities and villages were abandoned thousands of years ago and fell into disrepair.

In archaeology, context is essential to understanding the past because researchers often deal with prehistory—the undocumented past. Archaeologists rely on the placement of objects in an excavation site to offer insight into the way people lived. Similarly, according to Pinna, a historic house museum is fossilized if the furnishings, layout, and use of space are immutable. Pinna believes that "to alter them would be to falsify history."[6]

De Gorgas agrees. She calls it vital "to place the object[s] as much as possible in [their] original setting" to maintain the contextual integrity of the space.[7]

Over time, historic house museums are maintained—and in some cases updated—to look exactly as they once did. To alter the objects is to remove the context which they offer to the home, as well as their unique functions within the space. Visitors experience the historic house museum by experiencing the artifacts in space.

Learning by Looking
The majority of the learning for the visitor is done by looking, not through reading.

6   Giovanni Pinna. "Introduction to Historic House Museums," Museum International 53 (2001): 4-9.

7   De Gorgas, Mónica Risnicoff. "Reality as Illusion, the Historic Houses That Become Museums." *Museum Studies: An Anthology of Contexts*, 2nd ed., Wiley-Blackwell (2012): 324-328.

Not every visitor—especially younger ones—will read the wall plaques or object descriptions in a historic home. One could argue that, today, almost all learning can be done at home, on a computer or with a book. But there is a difference between seeing a photo of a George Washington's bedroom and standing there in the door of the room where he breathed his last breath. The bed, the room, the staircase with the low ceiling—all these things bring you into his world. You see the objects in the room as his things: the books in the library, the glasses on the table. The placement of objects throughout conveys how they were used and conveys something about the life of the person in the home—from canvases and paints in the study to cookie cutters in the kitchen.

The Risk of Forgetting the Past

Opening a historic home as a museum involves curating not only the objects, but also the narrative of the museum. Historic house museums are, in most cases are heritage sites: places to commemorate and exhibit a communal identity.

Something that is decisively worth preserving to a community must be an essential part of a collective history, identity, or narrative.

Consider the historic house museums in the Northeastern United States, like Mount Vernon and Monticello. Each year, thousands of students from across the country flock to these homes because they memorialize figures critical to the narrative of the nation's founding.

These homes "mirror the community"—especially around the time of the nation's founding—and "they are places in which the collective memory is created and preserves places where the members of these communities and nations find their own identity."[8]

These homes mirror a collective identity of which people are proud. As such, the identity or heritage which is put on display is carefully selected.

According to American historian David Lowenthal, humans "are bound to forget the past, but heritage leaves out far more than history."[9]

No one wants to identify with colonization and enslavement, and these realities are often sugarcoated in memorialization of famous colonial Americans. The heritage

8   Giovanni Pinna. "Introduction to Historic House Museums," Museum International 53 (2001): 4-9.

9   Lowenthal, David. "The Practice of Heritage." *The Heritage Crusade and the Spoils of History*, Free Press (1996): 148–172.

which Americans desire—the heritage conveyed in some museums and many textbooks—alters history. Shying away from difficult topics can be easy.

Lowenthal claims that "historians presume nothing should be forgotten" but often "deploy selective memory," altering our heritage enhanced by erasure in exhibit design and implementation.[10] Historians know what they have chosen to leave out, but—according to de Gorgas—visitors perceive every home as "true reality and therefore free of any kind of manipulation."[11]

People trust museums!

In a study by the American Association for State and Local History, 81 percent of respondents ranked history museums and historic sites as highly trustworthy. People believe these sites to be more trustworthy sources of information than history textbooks, nonfiction, high school history teachers, and even the internet.[12]

---

10 Ibid.
11 De Gorgas, Mónica Risnicoff. "Reality as Illusion, the Historic Houses That Become Museums." *Museum Studies: An Anthology of Contexts*, 2nd ed., Wiley-Blackwell (2012): 324–328.
12 Dichtl, John. "Most Trust Museums as Sources of Historical Information." AASLH, February 20, 2018.

From a young age, Americans are taught to trust textbooks and institutions. If a museum curator at Monticello claimed a book belonged to Thomas Jefferson, most visitors would believe them.

With this trust comes great responsibility, and that responsibility is to not fudge the past.

Presentist reshaping is the process of reshaping and contextualizing information for modern audiences—a well-intentioned modification of the past, hopefully. Lowenthal says museums need to be wary of "presentist reshaping," but calls it "unavoidable."[13]

Lowenthal argues that historians can even improve collective heritage by "endowing the past with today's exemplary perspectives."[14] Every decision made by museum curators and interpreters serves to alter the truth in some way. Changing a historic house is not entirely negative, but part of history is lost with every alteration—no matter how carefully the alteration is made.

---

13 Lowenthal, David. "The Practice of Heritage." *The Heritage Crusade and the Spoils of History*, Free Press (1996): 148–172.

14 Ibid.

Lost to Time

Whether a historic house is touched or untouched, history gets lost to time. The patina of age is unavoidable.

Museums change every day. They change intentionally by bringing in new exhibitions and doing more to stay relevant in the modern era—more on this in "The Activist."

But they are also victims to age—from repairing floors traipsed upon by thousands of visitors and patching leaky roofs to updating permanent exhibitions due to outdated technology.

Change, in any aspect, is inevitable. For historic house museums, there are all kinds of change. Some museums change intentionally by updating and meeting new building codes, for instance. Some react against change, perhaps by ignoring new codes or new cultural progressions. Museums also changed unintentionally from the simple passage of time and patina of age.

For historic house museums, the passage of time shows on the building and its objects, but at some point, this wear borders on serious deterioration. In some cases, renovation becomes dire: a foundation may need repairs to prevent collapse, a home may need new wiring to prevent a fire hazard. Modification is often not for aesthetic purposes, but rather out of necessity. Museums aim to preserve "the historical material" while "[keeping] the site as original to the period as possible"—even if that means adding anachronistic safety features.[15]

At the Moody Mansion in Galveston, Texas, a recent project to install fire sprinklers looks quite dissonant against the mansion's detailed, hand-painted ceiling. The red exit signs were surely not part of the original home, either.

These updates, though anachronistic, are crucial for protecting the past. The devastating 2018 fire at Brazil's National Museum exemplifies what can happen when a museum fails to update safety measures. More on this incident in Chapter 9.

Historic house museums must be kept in good condition—the challenge is to maintain them without sacrificing the historical integrity of the museum.

15   Barto, Jillian. "The New House Museum: How the Development of Modern House Museums Are Changing the Philosophies and Standards of Interpretation and Preservation." 2012.

Come Back Anytime

De Gorgas asserts, "We may return tirelessly to the events of the past, but they cannot be recovered in a definitive and well-defined way...in any single instance of return."[16]

No matter how fossilized the historic house museum may seem, every visitor imposes his or her own knowledge and experiences on the heritage site. Historians can only attempt to convey a unified idea of the past through exhibition design in a historic house museum. Ultimately, historic house museums are more intriguing when they leave the job of interpreting to the visitors— they will likely do that anyway.

---

16   De Gorgas, Mónica Risnicoff. "Reality as Illusion, the Historic Houses That Become Museums." *Museum Studies: An Anthology of Contexts*, 2nd ed., Wiley-Blackwell (2012): 324–328.

Part 3

The Curator

Chapter 8

Layers of Meaning

"You can find the entire cosmos lurking in its least remarkable objects."

—WISŁAWA SZYMBORSKA, POLISH POET

In some respects, many objects on display in museums are completely unremarkable on their own: rock samples, antelope fossils, and old pairs of shoes. The context shared alongside objects in an exhibition is what makes them beautiful and enchanting: not just a rock sample, but a sample of the moon which mankind traveled thousands of miles into outer space to pick up and bring home. Not just antelope fossils, but fossils found on the same site where an ancient human ancestor once lived and first began to walk on two legs. Not just an old pair of shoes, but the iconic, ruby-red slippers that graced the feet of Judy Garland in *The Wizard of Oz.*

"How can we even exhibit an object if we cannot communicate its full meaning?" Lauren Reid, anthropologist and co-director of the Insitu Collective, says, "Effectively conveying the layers of meaning and significance in an object" is ultimately the museum curator's dilemma.[1] Which stories do you choose to tell? Every object, no matter the age, has hundreds of layers of meaning and a variety of ways to look at it.

Reid believes museums should stop trying to convey the full meaning of objects and "instead open up their multiple realities."[2]

One story in context can add a new layer of beauty to artifacts, sure, but imagine trying to pull apart the seemingly-infinite perspectives of one object.

Let's do it.

***

Think about a penny. What's the first thing that comes to mind? What does it mean to you? What might it mean to others? What would you say about it if you put it on display? Depends on the context, right?

---

1   Reid, Lauren. "The Secret Life of Objects: Strategies for Telling New Stories in Exhibitions." Allegra, September 16, 2018.

2   Ibid.

There's that word again. Context.

What kind of museum would the penny go in? Trick question, it could go in any museum—if given the right context. To test this exercise, I found an object in my home—a penny—and attempted to decontextualize it. Everyone is walking around with a different perspective and unique set of experiences, so this penny could have an entirely different meaning to someone else. It could also have no meaning at all.

Penny, 1995

Looking for an object to start this exercise, the first thing I spotted was a penny, a small US coin, minted in 1995. A simple item like a penny can mean so much across various perspectives—it hardly means anything monetarily speaking.

Did you know it costs more money to produce a penny than it is actually worth?[3]

I've included the date of production for this particular coin for the sake of detail and context. Detail like this would presumably be included on an object label in a

---

3   United States Mint. 2010. *United States Mint annual report*. Washington, D.C.: U.S. Mint.

museum. The date of a penny carries a great deal of meaning and context with it—it asks the observer to consider what was happening in the world at the time of its minting.

What happened in 1995? O.J. Simpson's first trial came to an end, the first African American astronaut walked in space, the first planet outside our solar system was found, Windows 95 was released—I was still two years away from even existing.

Even though a penny minted today would look exactly the same, 1995 represents, for me, a sort of 'time before.' It represents the time before not only my existence, but also before the constant fear of terrorism that has defined the United States in the twenty first century. While 1995 was the year of the Oklahoma City bombing, it was still over half a decade before that infamous, fall day in New York City that shook the nation forever.

My mind was not immediately drawn to the monetary value upon selection of the item. A penny represents America to me even in its smallness. What stuck out to me, instead, was the phrase engraved on the backside of the coin—*e pluribus unum*. I remember learning in grade school that this Latin phrase translates to *out of many, one*. The age at which I learned this fact represents a great deal about the American school system and nationalist pride in America, at least in 2006.

To me this phrase, *e pluribus unum*, represents the unity of the American nation, despite its many discrete states. This motto is engraved on our currency as a constant reminder of the idealism that instigated the birth of our nation—a positivistic view I believe is worth preserving.

For others, however, this phrase may represent an obsolete belief of a once-proud nation. Many view the penny itself as an obsolete form of currency. Some look at the penny and see a nation run on the principles of capitalism. This small coin contains many layers of meaning and has been preserved throughout the nation's history despite many attempts to cancel its production.

***

Consider this mini-curatorial exercise a moment to reflect about yourself and what you value.

Try it with any object. Pick an item and consider all the ways it might be meaningful to you or others in your culture. Why would someone buy it? Why would someone hold on to it? Why would someone put it in a museum? Try it with a partner, or maybe try it in your next exhibit.

How radical would it be to create an exhibit about one object—perhaps an object that lacks universal significance—and unpack what that object means to all types of people, from all ages and walks of life. Even a small object can carry so much meaning with it—but an object only carries the meaning which we assign it.

Without context, it's just some copper-plated zinc.

Chapter 9

No Thing is Permanent

Nothing Gold Can Stay by Robert Frost

Nature's first green is gold,
Her hardest hue to hold.
Her early leaf's a flower;
But only so an hour.
Then leaf subsides to leaf.
So Eden sank to grief,
So dawn goes down to day.
Nothing gold can stay.

I remember calling my mother as soon as I switched to CNN in a total panic.

How did this happen? Was the whole thing going to burn down? Watching the spire fall was absolutely gut-wrenching. I didn't understand why it hurt so much. I'm neither French nor Catholic, so why was this place so important to me?

In April of 2019, Notre Dame de Paris unexpectedly caught fire in the middle of the day. The fire raged for several hours, completely destroying major components of one of the most famous cathedrals in the world.

To me, the cathedral is iconic, beautiful, and formidable. I always assumed it would just be there forever. It was here long before me, and I assumed it would exist long after. Perhaps that's what hurt the most—realizing the fleeting nature of even the most towering objects.

***

The good news is that Notre Dame did not burn down entirely, but the cathedral did suffer significant damage. Another piece of good news is that investigators found no sign of foul play or arson.[1] But is that really good news? Were there not safety measures in place to keep the fire from raging as it ultimately did?

In September 2018, Brazil suffered a similar tragedy and far greater loss. The National Museum of Brazil—"one of the richest collections of natural history artifacts in the world"—was largely destroyed by an accidental fire. The

---

1   Leasca, Stacey. "Officials Say These Two Things May Have Caused Notre Dame Fire." Travel Leisure, June 28, 2019.

fire consumed nearly the entire collection.[2] Since the fire, archaeologists, paleontologists, and other museum staff have been digging through the rubble to recover collection items—or what remains of them.

"The loss of the collection of the National Museum is incalculable to Brazil. Two hundred years of work, research and knowledge have been lost." - Michel Temer, president of Brazil[3]

The scale of the fire, however, could have been avoided. Investigators say the fire was caused by the installation of a new air conditioning system. The building also lacked the proper fire safety equipment to contain the flames.[4] The fire may have been caused by a single spark, but the total destruction of the National Museum was a product of decades of neglect according to Gustavo Pacheco, who graduated from the museum's anthropology doctoral program. "In 1999, when I started my Ph.D., the museum already had this aura

---

2   Chacoff, Alejandro. "Brazil Lost More Than the Past in the National Museum Fire." The New Yorker. The New Yorker, September 16, 2018.

3   Temer, Michael. Twitter Post. September 3, 2018, 5:59 PM.

4   "Air-Conditioning System Caused Brazil Museum Fire, Say Police." The Japan Times, April 5, 2019.

of decay, it was already full of termites," remembers Pacheco.[5]

It is massively important for museums to take care of their collections and the buildings that house them if they want the collections to last for future generations. Everything is always in decay, but plenty of actions can be taken to slow that decay. Like a fresh coat of paint on your house or Botox in your cheeks, museum conservators dedicate their careers to restoring and preserving artifacts.

Ellen Moody has been an art conservator at the Museum of Modern Art in New York for nearly a decade. Moody describes the daily tasks of a conservator as a combination of reactive work, like cleaning and repairing, and proactive work on the art—like advising crates for transport, putting up stanchions, and controlling the environment where art is displayed.[6] Conservators require a great deal of hyper-specific training, running the gamut from the sciences to the humanities—even skills in studio art. Not only is the degree difficult to achieve, but a job in art conservation is equally diffi-

5   Chacoff, Alejandro. "Brazil Lost More Than the Past in the National Museum Fire." The New Yorker. The New Yorker, September 16, 2018.

6   Moody, Ellen. YouTube. "LIVE Q&A with MoMA Painting & Sculpture Conservators Ellen & Diana (March 14)." The Museum of Modern Art, March 14, 2018.

cult to land. Collections are valued at anywhere from a few thousand dollars to utterly priceless, and handling them—let alone performing work on them—is a lot of responsibility.

I felt immensely stressed just watching a video of a conservation team handling the iconic *Starry Night*—holding my breath as they removed it from its 130-year-old frame.[7]

When you make changes to preserve something—an artifact or an entire building—you risk altering the object and its history. If you don't, however, you risk losing it entirely.

The task of the museum is to preserve objects and history, and no other facet of society can do this as effectively as museums.

Many people think museums are becoming obsolete now that we have the internet.

While I am a big fan of the internet, it cannot be the primary source of long-term preservation. Granted, technology has made preservation easier than ever before

---

7   YouTube. "Makes a Difference (S2, E6) | AT THE MUSEUM." The Museum of Modern Art, October 18, 2019.

for museums—but technology always has the possibility of crashing.

Picture this. Thousands of years from now, after we are long gone, an archeologist or some other being comes across an iPhone in the rubble of what used to be downtown Los Angeles. It doesn't turn on. The iPhone is now completely without context—only a little, black mirror and an empty battery.

"Digital storage, while magnificent, is not the savior of humanity or its artifacts."

—DAWSON FINKLEA, TECHNOLOGY CONSULTANT

The internet is great for sharing and digitizing collections for all to enjoy, nothing will ever surpass experiencing the collections in person.

"Museums are the only place where you can still see the real thing."

—RODNEY GENTRY, EXHIBIT DESIGNER AT THE
HOUSTON MUSEUM OF NATURAL SCIENCE

"To stand in front of these skulls and these bones is a really unique experience that you're not going to get from a flat little screen."

—JOHN MAISANO, EXHIBIT DESIGNER AT
THE TEXAS MEMORIAL MUSEUM

* * *

Physical systems of preservation do bring challenges. Physical preservation is hardly a perfect system. Even if the shelf life of brick-and-mortar museums is considerably longer than that of digital technology, nothing lasts forever.

Organic material decomposes from daily exposure to light, dust, and finger oils. Unforeseen accidents happen—everything from fire and flood to a painting being dropped.

So if nothing is permanent, and everything inevitably falls to decay—what's the point of preserving? Why prolong the inevitable?

The point of preserving is to prolong the inevitable so as many people as possible can enjoy the objects, artifacts, and their history. The artifacts can live on through memory and oral histories long after they disappear entirely.

Second death is a common concept in Hispanic culture and the root of many Day of the Dead traditions. Families build altars to those who've passed so that they can remember them and tell their stories.

"I mean, they say you die twice. One time when you stop breathing and a second time, a bit later on, when somebody says your name for the last time."

—BANKSY, STREET ARTIST[8]

Nothing in life is permanent. Museums come and go. New topic-based museums open annually, and even good museums sometimes close their doors for good. Some rebrand, bring in new ownership, or even rename themselves. Everything is always changing. Something new can always be discovered, preserved, or collected; something, too, is always deteriorating toward the point of irreparability.

***

---

8   Hogue, Adam. "Banksy Street Art: When Street Art Is in a Museum, What's the Point?" Mic, May 13, 2013.

The temporal nature of things doesn't have to be a total downer.

Angela Hall, director of learning at the Dallas Contemporary, talks passionately about a recent exhibit from Francesco Clemente. The artist came to the museum and hand-painted a mural on all four walls of the exhibit gallery. Hall says Clemente staunchly opposes capitalism and conceives of his murals as "art that can't be sold, only experienced."

Even though Clemente's murals must eventually be painted over for new exhibitions, Hall cherishes that Clemente's murals will "stay with us (the museum) forever"—resting beneath coats of paint, forever in the minds and hearts of those who experienced the exhibit.

"Once you recognize how fleeting and precious these moments are, you will appreciate them more."

—KATHERINE GARNER ON *NOTHING GOLD CAN STAY* BY ROBERT FROST[9]

***

9   Garner, Katherine. "Robert Frost's Nothing Gold Can Stay: Poem Meaning & Analysis." Study.com. Accessed September 8, 2019.

As I helplessly watched a global treasure burn before my eyes, I thought about the temporary nature of everything. Nothing lasts forever, nothing gold can stay—not even eight-hundred-year-old World Heritage sites.

This is not to be negative, however.

Through the many emotions I experienced in reaction to the burning of Notre Dame, I now understand the necessity to live in the present and cherish every day. Sure, nothing lasts forever, but don't focus on things that might end...enjoy them for what they are today. No one knows what tomorrow might bring.

Chapter 10

Too Small to Sit In

"The heart is a museum, filled with the exhibits of a lifetime's loves."

—*DIANE ACKERMAN, AUTHOR AND POET*

When I was barely two years old, my grandmother gave my mother an antique, child-sized rocking chair. You could tell by the way it was treated throughout the course of the object's life that it held little monetary value or even significance in memory. The chair was purely sentimental, an object you just couldn't throw away. Even after interviewing three members of my family, there were few memories to tell about this object. Even in its sparse mentions, the chair still managed to gain a rich history, especially in recent years.

The rocking chair stands about eighteen inches tall— small enough to fit a toddler, but no larger. The chair's form is simple with only the most basic components of a rocking chair and one horizontal, hand-carved piece across the back. What set this chair apart from the rest in my childhood home, however, was the hand-stitched, needlepoint pattern on the seat cushion. My great-great-grandmother stitched an image of a Dutch girl with a bonnet to personalize the chair for my family. She made the chair for my grandmother and her sister when they were very little, in the late 1940s. My mother says the chair itself might be even older.

My mother told me her mother and aunt frequently visited their grandparents' house, and—as far as she knew—the chair was not gifted on any particular occasion. The chair seemed to hold little significance even in the beginning. My great-great-grandmother simply made a chair for the girls to sit in when they visited. The missing link in my efforts to learn more about the chair is my grandmother, its first recipient—who sadly passed away when I was only six years old.

Even though my grandmother had a sister, they did not share the chair. It remained in my grandmother's home for many years—probably because her sister moved quite frequently. My grandmother owned the chair for the longest time, and her narrative will forever remain untold with regard to the object. When I asked my grandfather, her husband, about the rocker, he recalled little—it was, after all, primarily a matrilineal object. My father's response was very similar. Even my grandmother's sister, one of the chair's first recipients, remembers little to nothing about this family heirloom.

The next heir of the chair is my mother. The chair did not evoke particularly fond memories for her, either. She said the chair floated from one room to another in her childhood home and has done the same in her possession. My grandmother gifted my mother the chair when I, the first female grandchild, was nearly two years old. The chair was not actively involved in my mother's memories but it did, in a way, remind her of others: the joyful birth of her first child and the heart-breaking death of her mother.

The chair sat in the corner of my nursery for some time. It was also, at one point, the resting place for a porcelain doll in the living room of my parents' first apartment. When we moved into our first home in 1999, the chair moved around the house—as it continued to do in the house where I grew up.

So where's the story? When does this 'rich history' begin?

It begins with me, the object's biographer.

The rocking chair appears in my memory a handful of times. In one childhood memory, I was barely in kindergarten, but I remember the rocking chair sitting next to my kid-sized desk—complete with a plastic, yellow chair and clunky computer monitor. I never sat in the rocking chair because it was too short for my desk and seemed too delicate to be used. Occasionally, I would gently push the top half of the chair and watch it rock it back and forth, admiring the detailed needlework. As I traced the outline of the girl and her bonnet with my fingers.

We moved to our second home not long after I turned six years old. This new house was the home where I spent most of my childhood.

The rocking chair moved around to various corners of the house. It started in my parents' bedroom, next to another mid-century bench. My parents used that bench to stack my mother's excessive number of decorative pillows, which often spilled over onto the rocking chair. I remember its placement because I visited my parents' bedroom quite frequently. It was never an off-limits place for my brother and me—especially when my mom wanted help making the bed. She claimed to be teaching us a valuable skill—which is true, but as a kid it seemed unfair and tedious.

When I was in primary school, the chair sat right next to the piano in our dining room. My family does not come from money, and the piano was by no means grand. It looked like classic, americana furniture with light-colored wood and a few engraved, floral embellishments. The chair was right at home alongside it. I remember it there not because I interacted with it but because it was always present. Every day, for four years, I sat at the piano bench and practiced a craft I found frustrating at the time but would later come to appreciate. Every day, the chair sat in my peripheral view.

Occasionally my mom moved furniture around. She liked to mix things up, declutter, and practice her secret favorite hobby—interior decorating. In junior high, my mother decided the chair did not fit in any room of the house, so she stowed it in her closet. Recently, I asked why she hadn't put it in the attic, expecting some sentimental response, but she told me she kept it there to reach things on higher shelves.

In junior high, I took up sewing as a hobby. Every now and then, I would wander into my parents' closet and move the chair so I could rummage for supplies in my mother's sewing kit. The kit seemed to match the chair, almost as if they belonged together or were made by the same person.

The closet is the last place where I remember the chair before moving away for college. I had always thought it would remain there, frozen in time until I someday have a family of my own. Life, however, does not always play out as you might think.

In September 2017, our house flooded during a major hurricane. We lost nearly everything: the humble piano, the needlepoint bench, and the antique sewing kit. After the water receded, my family returned to rummage through the remains of the house where I grew up. My mother found the rocking chair nearly destroyed—the wood and cushion molded and the artwork separated from the seat. She managed to retrieve the rocking chair before flood remediation teams carelessly threw away what remained of our belongings.

Now, the house has been demolished, the lot sold, and my family relocated. For a while, what remained of the rocking chair sat quietly in the guest room of their new home in Galveston. The chair seemed caught in limbo: not important enough to display, left in arrested decay, but meaningful enough to keep and even salvage.

When I returned home for the first time after the disaster, my mother told me she wanted to repair the chair, keep as much of the original material as possible.

Among other reasons, she hoped to give it to me when I hopefully have a daughter someday.

After the hurricane, the chair was marked by tragedy. It finally had its shining moment, a momentous memory—even in its half-death. I so desperately wished to see it restored to its former glory. I had never given much thought to the chair in the past, but now I valued it immensely. While it was a symbol of a broken home—damaged by forces beyond our control—it was also a symbol of hope. Much like our family, it had the potential to be healed.

More than a year after the hurricane, I journeyed to my new home in Galveston for a much-needed break from my studies. I slumped up the stairs to my room after what seemed like an endless drive down the coast. As I set my things down, something seemed different. There it was, looking good as new: the little rocking chair. For my twenty-second birthday, my family banded together to bring the chair back to life. True to form, there it was—hidden in plain sight.

The chair after hurricane Harvey, 2017.

The chair restored, 2019.

Several things provide value to items of cultural heritage, like age and rarity. This chair may be almost worthless, but our family values it due to the memories and connotations it carries. When I was younger, the chair reminded me of new homes, births, deaths, and family ties. Now, the chair represents resilience in the face of adversity and perseverance through pain, suffering, and loss. There may not be much worth writing home about on the surface, but over time, the chair has collected its own set of memories and associations for each member of our family.

***

"The objects and the meaning we attach to things [change] our relationship to them."

—JOHNATHAN FEIN, FILMMAKER

The chair tells a story about a typical American, middle class, suburban family and a careful, observant girl.

Objects gain stories through their lives and through their interactions with humans. Our privilege is to tell them.

Museums chronicle, preserve, and share these stories with the public.

Come flood, famine, or societal collapse, we cling to our history for a sense of identity, of that which makes us human. Museums open and close each year, but we can take solace in one truth. Museums will never completely disappear because human nature will not allow it.

Part 4

The Skeptic

Chapter 11

Stuff

In grade school, a special speaker once visited for a school assembly. He gave us advice on writing essays.

"Never use the word 'stuff' when you write, unless you are talking about the inside of an Oreo."

After holding back for my entire academic career, I'm going to say it. Museums own a lot of stuff, display a lot of stuff, and are just full of stuff.

A museum without collections of objects is just a building. So far, we've seen several types of collections: books, inherited items, fossils, art, and more. We've seen that museums often get their start thanks to collectors and generous donations. Many collections are never formally institutionalized, and they may not be museums in the traditional sense—but they come pretty close.

Human nature is to collect things. Humans have a basic need to hunt, gather, and collect resources; after the Neolithic Revolution, however, humans began to build permanent homes and curate objects within them. For thousands of years, humans across the globe have adopted the practice of forming collections of very specific objects—from Fabergé eggs to toilet seats.

Toilet Seat Art museum in The Colony, TX

Collectors set themselves apart from the crowd as particularly creative and thoughtful people. Many humans understand their own basic needs, but individuals who collect look beyond necessity for a sense of greater joy.

Collection(s) (n.) are intentional gatherings of things that give people joy and often promote reflection or introspective thought.

Each object in a collection is a subtle reminder of the past—whether that past is personal, familial, or collective. People collect things they love to connect them to a personal past, other people, and physically host part of their identity.

Collecting is not hoarding. Collecting is thoughtful, organized, and intentional.

I, like many others, am a collector. I have an extensive collection of magnets from places I have visited and, of course, museums I've seen. I have criteria for the types of magnets I collect and the patterns by which I organize and display them. This time, however, I will turn to another thoughtful human to explore the nature of collecting.

A small portion of Laurel's collection of Funko Pop! dolls

Laurel collects *Funko Pop!* dolls—fun-sized, vinyl caricatures of famous characters from movies, literature, and American culture. These dolls serve no functional purpose and are by no means necessity. Like all personal collections, Laurel's is purely nostalgic.

Items in a collection are no longer for daily use. Some objects may have been used at one time, but no longer serve that purpose now that they belong to a collection.

The arrowheads at the National Museum of American History are no longer hurled at unassuming bison, and no one uses the telescope collection at Italy's Museo Galileo to map the cosmos.

A museum's collection often consists of hundreds of smaller collections, as well as a few noteworthy collections on permanent display. The public has the extraordinary benefit of learning from these preserved objects—preserved being the key word. Museums do not subject collections to the wear of daily use; instead, they keep them in good condition for future generations to study and enjoy.

Laurel's collection of *Funko Pop!* dolls is not as extensive as a museum collection. A humble, nomadic college student, her possessing a novelty collection is even more non-essential. College students can only lug their most treasured belongings about—this speaks to value and importance Laurel holds for her collection.

Laurel has about ten dolls, which she has collected over the past seven years. Originally from Dallas, Texas, Laurel only purchases her *Funko Pop!* dolls from a specific, local store, and never orders them online. Each doll represents a character from a piece of pop culture that she enjoys or admires. While several designs and hundreds of characters are available, Laurel has chosen only a select few. She has no desire to collect every doll, the rare dolls, or even her favorite characters. Instead, she picks the ones she likes, happens upon, or receives as gifts from her friends and family. Laurel has set these standards for her collection.

Museums have standards for collection items as well.

To help combat the massive collection in storage at The Indianapolis Museum of Art, curators at the museum developed a ranking system for the collection. Paintings and sculptures that don't meet their standards are systematically removed from the always growing collection.[1] In some cases, museums become dumping grounds for local collections of items; Texas Memorial Museum, for instance, has individual collections of spoons, watches, light fixtures, and teapots, all from various donors. There is so much stuff to share that many museums do not own collections. The Bullock Museum of Texas State History, for instance, holds its exhibit pieces on loan from other individuals and institutions.

Susan Stewart, American poet and professor of English at Princeton University, has written extensively on

---

1   Pogrebin, Robin. "Clean House to Survive? Museums Confront Their Crowded Basements." The New York Times, March 10, 2019.

human patterns of collecting. Stewart believes the selective nature of collections shows "eclecticism rather than pure seriality."[2] Laurel's collection standards, for instance, are a reflection of her identity in relation to each character. Collecting them all, in contrast, would be "pure seriality," as Stewart calls it. Laurel's collection is a physical representation of her specific interests in film and popular culture, not her interest in the doll's materiality. Her means of acquiring each doll allow for the formation of meaningful memories involving other people in her life. Purchasing online is a solo effort; and going to the mall or receiving gifts from family, in contrast, cultivates meaningful bonds.

Most of Laurel's *Funko Pop!* Dolls are from the Marvel comic franchise, of which she is an avid fanatic. Her obsession began when her uncle shared his collection of comic books with her; it has been growing ever since. Obsessions inspire collections, which in turn inspire obsessions that inspire more collections. Historian, scholar, and anthropologist James Clifford asserts, "Collecting is inescapably tied to obsession."[3]

---

2   Stewart, Susan. *On Longing: Narratives of the Miniature, the Gigantic, the Souvenir, the Collection*. Durham and London: Duke University Press, 1993.

3   Clifford, James. *The Predicament of Culture: Twentieth-century Ethnography, Literature, and Art*. Cambridge, MA: Harvard University Press, 2002.

Clifford goes on to say objects within collections are often "curiosities to be giggled at [or] art to be admired," as these *Funko Pop!* dolls are. Laurel's collection began with Loki, the primary villain of Marvel's *Thor* comics. Laurel bought this doll immediately following the release of *Thor* in 2011. She picked up the first doll because she really liked the movie, as well as the dynamic nature of Loki's character—but mostly because "it was just so cute."

Obsessive collectors have brought us many of the educational collections which we cherish today.

The Houston Museum of Natural Science has one of the largest collections of trilobite fossils thanks to a very enthusiastic collector by the name of Sam Stubbs. The museum also features an extensive collection of jewel-encrusted works by the House of Fabergé generously donated by Dorothy McFerrin.

Visual anthropology scholars Marita Sturken and Lisa Cartwright claim people often build collections based on "aesthetic reasons" and the value of each object "resides in the pleasure it brings us."[4] The Loki figurine appeals to Laurel visually and brings her joy in

---

4   Sturken, Marita, and Lisa Cartwright. *Practices of Looking: An Introduction to Visual Culture.* New York: Oxford University Press, 2001.

multiple ways—from trips to the mall with her friends to watching Marvel films with her family.

Laurel says she aims to "keep them where she can see them." In her childhood home, they were lined up against the windowsill. In her new apartment, however, the windowsill "sits too low and out of sight," so the dolls reside in three separate spots in her bedroom.

Laurel bases her arrangement of the dolls on newness, visual appeal, and meaning. Her dolls sit where she spends most of the time in that space: near her bed while she sleeps, at her desk while she works, and on her dresser while she prepares for the day.

Stewart says, "The spatial whole of the collection supersedes the individual narratives that lie behind it."[5]

The collection is a daily reminder of Laurel's identity.

"I'm a geek!" she claims. "This is me. I'm a Marvel fan."

Through consultation with experts in collecting, it seems collections form out of some level of selfishness—but not in a wholly negative sense.

---

5   Ibid.

Personal collections are self-centered and assist in self-reflection and self-identifying.

Personal collections are self-centered and the reasons for starting or having a collection are selfish and materialistic. People buy what pleases them and assists them in conveying their ideal reputation. I hardly need my collection of magnets, but it pleasures me and suggests my worldliness and love of travel.

Collections assist in self-reflection. Laurel's collection of figurines gives her the opportunity to consider how her collection adds to her character, what her character implies to observers, and the memories she associates with the fandom.

Collections assist in self-identifying. Laurel's collection is her way of telling people she is a Marvel fanatic. The objects in a collection, as well as their organization—according to Stewart—show more about the collector than the collection itself.[6]

Though selfishness and materialism may have negative connotations, none of these facets of collections are inherently negative.

---

6   Ibid.

Unique obsessions make the collection unique and provide insight into human behavior.

***

I invite you to think about what collections you might have: postcards, coins, stamps, stuffed animals, ticket stubs, t-shirts—the list is endless. Reflect on what your collections mean to you. Remember: a collection has organization and intention; it's something you likely enjoy sharing with others.

Chapter 12

The Importance of Context

Ozymandias by Percy Shelley

I met a traveler from an antique land,
Who said, "Two vast and trunkless legs of stone
Stand in the desert... Near them, on the sand,
Half sunk a shattered visage lies, whose frown,
And wrinkled lip, and sneer of cold command,
Tell that its sculptor well those passions read
Which yet survive, stamped on these lifeless things,
The hand that mocked them, and the heart that fed;
And on the pedestal, these words appear:
My name is Ozymandias, King of Kings;
Look on my Works, ye Mighty, and despair!
Nothing beside remains. Round the decay
Of that colossal Wreck, boundless and bare
The lone and level sands stretch far away."

Once, I was sitting in a coffee shop with a friend. We were chatting about museums. He showed me this poem, and as he read it to me, something began to emerge deep from the depths of my subconscious. I had heard this before in a high school English class some seven or eight years ago. We had read it together in class and discussed the idea of human legacy.

Humans desire to leave a legacy, to leave something behind, to be remembered. There are many reasons to write a book: to educate people on a specific topic, to preserve an oral history, to provide insight into a certain locale, perhaps. At its core, however, the act is pretty self-centered.

Yes, I did just call myself selfish.

Humans aren't here for long—nor, as a species, have we been here for more than a blink of the cosmic eye. Armed with the knowledge of our fleeting existence, we seek to leave a mark—some immortal legacy to compensate for the crushing weight of recognizing own mortality.

Ozymandias is no exception. Ozymandias is the Greek name for Rameses II, who was among the most revered pharaohs of the New Kingdom in ancient Egypt.

Around the time when Shelley wrote *Ozymandias*, the British Museum had just announced the acquisition of a partial granite statue of Rameses II. The museum had acquired the upper torso and bust of Rameses, but the rest of the statue had been lost to the sands. Shelley's poem, inspired by a museum visit, brings us to the site where those legs might have stood—granite monoliths immortalized in the sand.

"Tell that its sculptor well those passions read / Which yet survive, stamped on these lifeless things."

Museums are full of objects and contexts we place upon them. Curators attempt to tell the story for these lifeless objects. Where would we be, as viewers, without context?

"Nothing beside remains. Round the decay / Of that colossal Wreck, boundless and bare."

Even a pair of stone legs and a pedestal with an inscription is more context than a pair of legs alone. Imagine a museum full of objects, but wholly without object biographies.

How are we to know that things in museums hold intrinsic value? We assign value by the contexts we place on the objects. Without context, a thing only has meaning to its owner and the memories they attach to that object. This context, of course, dies with the owner.

This holds true in the case of Ozymandias. Archaeologists merely found a statue in the middle of a desert. Armed with knowledge of ancient Egypt and its history, however, they are able to tell us about this statue—a memorial to one of the most powerful rulers of the region.

Every bit of context will contain some opinion or perspective—this is the inherent danger in authoring an object biography. Every exhibition designer faces the challenge of the weight which their context will inevitably put on each piece in the collection. People tend to trust in museums, but how are we to evaluate the contexts with which curators provide us?

Museum professionals have the freedom to portray artifacts as they wish. With this freedom, however, comes great responsibility. Museum professionals also have a responsibility to their community: to be, informative, not necessarily truthful.

What would a museum be without the context provided by curators? A sort of garage sale, filled with meaningless items? A storage unit? It would not inform—it would just exist.

Context is key to our understanding. The job of museum professionals is to curate exhibits and provide us with context through which we can better understand those exhibits.

Chapter 13

Everything is Trash

"Experience is the teacher of all things."

—*JULIUS CAESAR*

Rodney Gentry, exhibit designer at the Houston Museum of Natural Science, has an unpopular opinion.

"Nothing in here is worth anything," he says, standing in the grand hall of the HMNS. "The museum is full of trash. Everything in the museum was trash at one time or another."

My entire world was turned upside-down.

He could clearly see the look of shock on my face and went on to explain that several artifacts were donations—things people did not want enough to keep in their home or items left behind by someone's passing. Archaeological dig sites, he went on to explain, also come up with artifacts like broken pottery from the trash piles of ancient villages.

Gentry might have a point. Now, everywhere I go, I look at an artifact and wonder: why did the museum find this worthy of display? Is this valuable to anyone?

They say one man's trash is another man's treasure.

So, everything is trash, and nothing is.

If everything is trash, why have museums? Why are things displayed in museums?

Utility

Things are sometimes displayed in museums because they have served a functional purpose in life; they were useful to humans in some way.

For example, you might go to see an exhibit on pottery that was excavated from an archaeological site. Much of that pottery, however, is probably the equivalent of dishware from IKEA: purely functional and not extravagant. Objects like these serve a utilitarian purpose. By putting them on display, however, a museum educates its patrons about past cultures: how people made the artifact, the materials they used from their environment, and what they ate or stored within it.

Gentry says once, when he was traveling in Latin America, he was served guacamole in a five-hundred-year-old bowl by one host. Gentry wondered why the object hadn't been placed in a museum. His host had a simple response, "Because it's in my fridge."

The artifact is still serving a utilitarian purpose; it remains an active part of someone's life. Artifacts can hardly enter into museums until their owner is finished with them. Your iPhone X, for instance, might be displayed in a local science museum someday.

Artifacts can also have ceremonial value—they are useful, but not every day. The Crown Jewels of the United Kingdom are displayed in the Tower of London, not worn daily by the queen. The crown serves a purpose in specific moments of note—otherwise, it sits on display for millions of tourists to wonder over.

Ceremonial objects in museums teach visitors about tradition; they invite them to understand other cultures through the meaning which certain objects hold in those cultures.

Aesthetics

Ceremonial objects sit midway between functional and aesthetic objects. They serve a function, sometimes. Aesthetic objects exist on the opposite end of the spectrum from utilitarian objects.

Artifacts with aesthetic value are looked at, not used—like art. You wouldn't typically pick up a painting and hammer something into the wall with it. Art is to be experienced. Objects that have aesthetic value are looked at and learned from. They are displayed for reasons including rarity, quality, and condition.

Pieces of art on display often exemplify a unique category, time period, or method. The splatter paintings of Jackson Pollock are just one example. Pollock's work is unique because he tried something new—his art teaches us about human movement and emotional expression through random bursts of paint.

Some items are displayed for their rarity. The Hope Diamond—on display at the National Museum of Natural History in Washington, DC—is rare because of its blue hue and size. The enormity of this diamond teaches us something new about how gemstones are formed.[1]

---

1   "Gems and Minerals – Beauties and Building Blocks." Smithsonian National Museum of Natural History. Accessed November 8, 2019.

Backstory

Things can also have value through their attachment to memory. Objects hold different levels of value for different people, depending on their knowledge of the object's backstory.

Portions of bent, melted beams from the World Trade Center in New York City are on display at the Newseum in Washington, DC. The beams memorialize a traumatizing time for citizens of New York City and the nation; they teach visitors about a defining moment in history for the United States. The backstory gives meaning and value to the object.

The *Mona Lisa*, for instance, derives some of its value from its history. The painting has been stolen, twice. With an estimated worth of over eight hundred million dollars, the painting has the highest insurance value of any artifact in the world.[2]

No one thought much of the painting before it was stolen in 1911. According to Blake Gopnik, a writer for the Washington Post, the *Mona Lisa* was "just another Leonardo until early last century, when the scandal of

---

2   "Highest Insurance Valuation for a Painting." Guinness World Records. Accessed November 8, 2019.

the painting's theft from the Louvre and subsequent return kept a spotlight on it over several years."[3]

Often, the story of an artifact's journey is more remarkable than the object itself.

* * *

Objects are put on display for a multitude of reasons, but all serve some educational function. They teach us about cultures, chemical processes, or noteworthy persons or events in human history.

The most valuable things of all are not the objects themselves, but rather the experiences that the objects foster.

Museums foster experiences through things.

* * *

Take a moment to ask yourself or someone nearby: what is the most valuable museum object you recall? What museum artifact do you remember best? What artifact would you love to see? What would you put in a museum?

---

3   Gopnik, Blake. "A Record Picasso And the Hype Price of Status Objects." The Washington Post. WP Company, May 7, 2004.

Chapter 14

Reproducing Icons

In the summer of 2009, my mom left the country for the first time to visit London and celebrate a birthday milestone. She brought back small gifts for everyone: cufflinks for my dad, pins for my brother, and three magnets for me.

I had never left the country, or gone anywhere too terribly exciting—outside of Disney World—at that point in my life. I was only twelve. I had dreamed of going to Paris since I was a kid. Something about the history, music, and architecture called out to me. I sat at my desk in the presence of these three magnets from historic sites in London. My fascination with these three magnets later prompted an obsession with collecting magnets from every place I went.

Others caught wind of this collection, but that was expected since the wall of magnets was hard to miss for anyone who set foot in my room. In junior high and high school, close friends would sometimes bring back magnets from their travels for me: Las Vegas, New York, Venice Beach, and Park City. My parents, too, brought me back a magnet from every business trip: Alaska, Chicago, Memphis, and three more visits to London.

Nearly every place I went—and every museum I visited—I brought home a magnet, if I could find one.

I like magnets best of all souvenirs. When I was younger, I proudly displayed each magnet in my room—careful to arrange them in thoughtful patterns and categories. Eventually, the collection grew so large that it occupied my entire closet door. Each magnet had a memory attached to it: a maple leaf from Niagara Falls, a sea otter from a very rainy family vacation to Seattle, and a corkscrew from a kiosk outside the statue of David in Florence.

I look at my magnet collection as others might view old home movies. Each magnet serves as a little reminder of a moment I might otherwise forget. A good number of these magnets are from museums, of course. Museum shops were usually the place to find them—outside of airports and gas stations.

At museums, I usually buy magnets of famous exhibit pieces: a small sculpture of King Tut, a wooden panel of the Rosetta Stone, and tiny ceramic fresco of the Creation of Adam. What happens to the perceived value of these cultural objects when you reproduce them and take them home?

Value is something that we as a society collectively place on things—or a human construct.

The perceived value of an object is how much an individual believes it is worth. Perceived value varies from person to person; many things, however, have intrinsic value to society as a whole. Society has, in other words, agreed on their value—those things typically end up in museums. These objects of societal worth then become popularized and consequently commodified.

The word 'commodified' carries a certain negative connotation, but reproducing these treasures allows people to bring the extraordinary into their everyday lives. Revenue from souvenirs also helps to keep museums open—especially those with free admission—and allows people to admire items of cultural significance more often.

Many academics would disagree, however. They take issue with the devaluation of objects through diminutive reproductions. Mary Beard, professor of Classics at the University of Cambridge, says "shallow material culture" has been part of museums since the beginnings of the institution, particularly at the British Museum.[1]

All museums celebrate some kind of identity: of a time, a region, a place, or an individual. The British Museum is a historical museum and, as such, celebrates the once all-powerful British Empire. The British Museum houses a host of objects from cultural groups across space and time. More about the controversial means by which the museum obtained these objects can be found in chapters six and twenty-four.

The Rosetta Stone is known worldwide for its linguistic significance. Scholars were able to use the stone to decipher hieroglyphics because it includes three different languages on its face: hieroglyphic script, ancient Egyptian, and ancient Greek. Beard, however, argues the reverence given to the Rosetta Stone in the modern day is a prime example of "shallow material culture."[2]

---

1 Beard, Mary. "Souvenirs of Culture: Deciphering (in) the Museum." *Art History* 15, no. 4 (December 1992): 505–32.

2 Ibid.

People travel from far and wide just to see the Rosetta Stone. Beard notes, however, that people often only glimpse at the stone for a few seconds—and I can attest to that truth.

My first trip to the British Museum was not too long ago. A budding anthropologist, I was beyond excited to see thousands of years of human history under one roof. I could hardly contain myself. When I entered the room with the Rosetta Stone, my soul left my body, took a trip around the cosmos, and landed right back in my chest. You might think people spend hours waiting their turn to see the stone, but I waited a mere thirty seconds to be right up against the glass.

Why travel all that way to see the stone, take a glance, and move on? The museum has been free since its opening in 1753,[3] so perhaps people worry less about staying awhile. The gift shop, however, is not free. It's filled with magnets, pins, postcards, scarves—just about every possible way to commodify the Rosetta Stone. People purchase these items all day long.

Does this practice of commodification diminish the perceived value of the Rosetta Stone? Do people spend

3   "History of the British Museum." The British Museum. Accessed September 14, 2019.

less time with the real stone because they can take one home, look it up on the internet later? Maybe. Perhaps this practice is also related to the diminishing modern attention span.

* * *

Though Beard criticizes the odd choices in postcard iconography, she recognizes "the necessary commercialism" of souvenirs in the modern museum.[4]

Museums run on tourism and material culture. The going, seeing, and then buying keeps them open and, consequently, accessible.

But Beard criticizes the attitude of seeing simply for the sake of seeing in the modern day. Going simply to see—and not to feel, experience, or learn—is far too superficial, she believes.[5]

It might be nice for every visitor to appreciate every artifact, as would an anthropologist or art historian, but this expectation is unrealistic. Each person is an individual with individual thoughts, feelings, and ideals.

---

4   Beard, Mary. "Souvenirs of Culture: Deciphering (in) the Museum." *Art History* 15, no. 4 (December 1992): 505–32.

5   Ibid.

You cannot force people to take an interest in something, but you can certainly help make things more interesting.

This is where the role of a museum educator becomes vital. Learning about an item—why it is held in such high regard, for instance—allows for a far more enriching and enlightening experience. Museum educators, in this way, add depth to the material culture espoused within museum gift shops. Context is the solution to the shallow nature of going and seeing.

***

What do you picture when you hear the word 'tourist'?

Tourist typically carries some negative connotations—an online search for news about tourists will reveal that truth pretty quickly.

Everyone, however, has been a tourist somewhere at some point—yet we refuse to believe we fall into this category. I will admit I often fall prey to the appeal of souvenirs, but tourists are the unsung heroes of the industry. Tourists spend their hard-earned money to travel thousands of miles to see these museums and artifacts.

***

The next time you are a tourist in a museum, I challenge you to be more considerate and intentional. I challenge you to put down the camera and, instead, try to be present with the object. Be thoughtful about what you see in front of you. Perhaps the exhibit will become so etched in your brain that you won't feel the need to take a picture. At any rate, you can always mosey over to the gift shop and take home a reproduction of the object to enjoy every day.

Part 5

The
Businessman

Chapter 15

Show Me the Money!

"Donors don't give to institutions. They invest in ideas and people in whom they believe."

—G.T. 'BUCK' SMITH, FUNDRAISING
CONSULTANT FOR HIGHER EDUCATION

Museums are businesses.

Some are for profit. Some are not-for-profit.

Some are run by local or national governments. Some are private.

Some museums have multi-million-dollar operating budgets. Some do not.

Most museums are 501(c)(3) organizations—public charities, or, more commonly, nonprofits. Sotheby's Institute of Art warns, however, that "nonprofit is a tax status, not a business plan"—making a profit is, in fact, essential to operation. This tax status allows museums to avoid corporate income tax on their revenue—as long as their earnings go toward mission-driven expenses and employee salaries. [1]

Public charities are still businesses, and they require budget-minded leaders and accounting professionals to survive, just like any other business. Museums do not sell a product for the sole advancement of the corporation, however—they provide education for the greater good of the public. Museums, however, still have to sell themselves to donors and to the public.

Museum profits come from a few places. The smallest contribution comes from ticket sales. Even though it costs twenty-five dollars for a ticket to the Metropolitan Museum of Art, which sees over seven million visitors annually, ticket sales only account for a mere 2% of their overall revenue.[2] The largest part of a museum's revenue, seems to just fall out of the sky on the wings of angels: the donors.

---

1   "The Business Model of the Nonprofit Museum." Sotheby's Institute of Art. Accessed September 28, 2019.

2   Ibid.

Contributions from donors typically account for over half of a museum's revenue.[3]

> ## "A nonprofit is owned by society."
> —CARL HAMM, FORMER FUNDRAISING EXECUTIVE
> AT THE SAINT LOUIS ART MUSEUM

Typically, when you spend money on something, you own it. On the surface, a donation might look like a gift without strings attached, but there is occasional puppetry involved. Carl Hamm has thirty years of fundraising experience and has spent much of his career raising money for museums and other cultural institutions. When Hamm told the crowd at the Texas Association of Museums Fundraising Conference that "a nonprofit is owned by society," every museum representative in the room nodded.

Museums are for the public and funded by the public.

The audience of a museum has a great deal of influence over what the museum displays because museums want to bring people in the door. Donors have a great deal of influence over museums because their gifts account for sixty percent of revenue, on average.[4] The influence

---

3 Ibid.
4 Ibid.

that visitors and donors have may not always be direct, but museum administrators rely on more visitors and repeat donors to survive. Museum actions, therefore, are decisively influenced by society.

The Modern Leisure Market

According to the American Alliance of Museums, there are about 850 million visits to American museums each year—nearly double the number of visits to all major sporting events and theme parks combined.[5]

Museums have always been a part of the tourism industry. Recently, however, exhibit designers, marketing visionaries, and programming professionals are creating exhibits and activities that move museums closer to the entertainment industry. Zoe Ingram, director of strategic projects at the Rock and Roll Hall of Fame, explains that modern museums have one foot in each industry: tourism and entertainment. Museums are part of the modern leisure market—how people spend money in their free time.

Competition for public attention encourages change and growth in museums. In the modern day, museums

---

5   "Museum Facts & Data." American Alliance of Museums, December 11, 2018.

compete with attractions like theme parks, and exhibit designers are rising to the challenge by making exhibit halls as exciting as the queue lines at Disney World.

In the last decade, museums have also faced another competitor: the internet. Why go to a museum or a library for information when the world is at your fingertips? Museum professionals have responded by helping their museums go digital. No longer do you need to leave your own home to visit a museum or peruse a collection—a revolution in the accessibly of material. However, the internet is not a competitor but a tool through which museums can reach broader audiences. The Met, the Smithsonian, the Field Museum, the Getty—museums that remain hundreds of miles apart are now just a click away.

If a membership isn't already appealing enough, program executives are developing more community events that are often free for members. Some programs are mission-driven, like lectures and workshops; some, too, are more creative, allowing the museum to serve as a community center. London's Natural History Museum offers yoga practices in the grand hall, hosts a massive event for New Year's Eve—even silent disco on the weekends. The Houston Museum of Natural Science often sells out of tickets for its Night and the Museum event;

the museum has also been known to host happy hour libations in the fossil hall.

These events, though, enticing, pale in comparison to the annual fundraising gala—the biggest revenue event of the year. Not every museum hosts an annual gala since they are a feat of organization and sometimes more trouble than they're worth. Unless, of course, you're the Metropolitan Museum of Art.

***

The Met has a leg up on most museums—a few million legs up, really.

Monetarily, the most successful museums often have three things in common: size, location, and age. The biggest players in the industry have existed for centuries and host extensive collections. Museums in large metropolitan areas are also more accessible and more visible—with plentiful resources and tourism to boot.

The age of a museum cannot be expedited.

A museum can launch a capital campaign, open a second location, or relocate entirely, but a museum cannot accelerate time. Age matters because the longer a museum has existed, the more it has exhibited—the more lives it has touched, and the more donors it fosters.

Museums cannot survive without revenue.

When governments cut budgets for art and culture, museums have to let staff go, reduce hours, and sometimes close entirely. Worse still—as in the case of the National Museum of Brazil—budget cuts can lead to near-total destruction of the museum through failure to update safety systems.

Donations generally do not go toward general operations or facility updates but toward flashier, public programs. Entire collections—hundreds of years of human history, cores to our collective identity—are at stake when museums do not have effective financial support.

Many museums ask for nothing but your time. If you take the time to visit, you might just be convinced to open your pocketbook.

Chapter 16

Size Doesn't Matter

"...the very thing that gave the giant his size was also the source of his greatest weakness."

—MALCOLM GLADWELL, DAVID AND GOLIATH

Bigger is not always better.

Large museums have enormous operating budgets but not every large museum I've visited has taken advantage of the wide array of resources to enhance visitor experience in the modern era. Some large museums are as they always have been since their initial opening.

You've probably been in a museum that seems like a silent, intimidating maze. Collections like these might be impressive, sure, but they sometimes fail to make things all that interesting.

If you have a particular museum in mind, ask yourself: can you remember a single artifact you saw?

A successful museum adventure, to me, always gives me something new—a memorable experience or something learned.

A museum does not have to be hundreds of thousands of square feet, or even one square foot, to accomplish this.

"MICRO is building a fleet of six-foot-tall museums."[1] MICRO, an innovative museum startup, has built two interactive pod museums as of 2019—stationing them in public places, like New York's Rockefeller Center. At South by Southwest, an annual music festival in Austin, Texas, MICRO recently took home a Place by Design Award.

Though only a few square feet, MICRO is bringing high-quality science to the thousands who pass by their exhibits each day.

Believe it or not, some museums take up no physical space at all.

---

1   "About." MICRO. Accessed October 22, 2019.

Girl Museum has been around for the last decade. Where? Nowhere.

Girl Museum has run some fifty-two exhibitions thus far without holding collections or maintaining a physical space. Instead, the museum draws on open-access collections, partnerships with other museums, and volunteers to run a museum through a simple website.[2]

"Being virtual also promotes inclusivity in who can visit: anyone with a computer and internet connection," remarks Tiffany Rhoades Isselhardt, program developer for Girl Museum. "The twenty-first-century museum—with its focus on serving people—does not necessarily need a physical presence to fulfill its mission."[3]

With an online platform called Virmuze, you can explore a network of virtual museums and even make your own digital museum.[4]

Girl Museum and Virmuze exhibit collections through blog posts, images, and interactive maps. Three-dimensional digital museums exist, too.

---

2   Isselhardt, Tiffany Rhoades. "Collecting Girlhood: Why the New Activist Museum Is Virtual." American Alliance of Museums, April 9, 2019.

3   Ibid.

4   "About." Virmuze. Accessed October 22, 2019.

Valentino Garavani Museum is a downloadable desktop app where you can wander through the halls of a digital museum filled with five decades of sketches, videos, and images of the fashion designer's work.[5]

***

"With decreased funding, increased competition, and the burden of care, museums have to reimagine themselves," says Isselhardt.

Plenty of museums deviate from the traditional mold. Physical space may provide room to grow, but physical limitations are not stopping museum innovators.

---

5   Team, BoF. "Inside Valentino Garavani's Virtual Museum." The Business of Fashion, December 7, 2011.

Chapter 17

Money Matters

"An investment in knowledge pays the best interest."

—BENJAMIN FRANKLIN

During my time at university, I gained a great deal of knowledge and insight into the curation, fundraising, and collection work that leads to successful museums. I also spent a great deal of time wandering the halls of on-campus exhibits, as well as just about any museum I could find—near or far.

To say I am a museum enthusiast would be a polite understatement. I am a complete museum nerd. My idea of a vacation includes a packed day of cultural sights and experiences.

As I combined my collegiate studies with casual museum adventures, I found myself contemplating the ethics and management of museums more frequently. Once a thing or object in a museum gains context, new issues can arise about rightful ownership and monetary value.

Before the in-depth reading assignments and personal exhibition tours, I was very provincial in my thinking about the museum experience as a whole. I was only a tourist.

Tourists perpetuate what classics professor Mary Beard calls 'go and see' culture. Tourists go to appreciate simply the item, but not its surrounding context. This behavior, however, ultimately, keeps museums in business.[1]

I had not previously thought of museums as business until I sat down with former director of the National Museum of American History, John Gray. Gray's background in finance offers him a unique understanding of what it takes for museums to succeed. Gray's background allows his observations about museums as institutions to be less fantastical and more empirical.

"Finance isn't just accounting. It's the idea of how organizations work; what strategies work, what brand identity

---

1   Beard, Mary. "Souvenirs of Culture: Deciphering (in) the Museum." Art History 15, no. 4 (1992): 505-532.

is about, what motivates people, what are the economic forces in the world," says Gray.

When I was younger, my parents took me to museums—which, even then, seemed like playgrounds of learning and imagination. Kids don't consider what it takes to assemble a museum, but they do enjoy them. I think the same could be said for most visitors and tourists. Adults might be more critical than children but are there to enjoy the exhibitions all the same. Gray and others in his industry, in contrast, see the museum as a business—living and thriving in the tourism industry.

I expect to pay a fee to see an exhibition.

In fact, I wasn't even aware students could receive free admission to certain institutions until college. As a child, I had never considered why museums charged fees—it was just a fact of life. More often than not, I also was not the one footing the bill—lemonade stands and lawn-mowing just weren't cutting it.

In January of 2018, I went on a class visit to Texas Memorial Museum (TMM) in Austin, Texas. I hadn't been to this museum since I was very young, and we were fortunate enough to receive a private tour and discussion with museum staff. Pamela Owen, the associate director at the time, mentioned the addition of an admission fee in light of recent budget cuts. According to Pamela, the museum was free to the public from 1937 through 2014.

In an ideal world, it would have remained free. But institutions require money to function.

Where does that money come from? Sometimes, the government—this, however, is not the case for the Texas Memorial Museum.

The museum's budget shrunk significantly after the preceding legislative session in Texas, and they have even received warning of plans to cut funding entirely. It seems odd to me that Texas would even consider throwing away such a precious piece of state history: the Texas Memorial Museum was the first state history museum for Texas, and it would be a true shame to see it go. I began to better understand the outdated nature of some exhibits at the TMM. It takes money to maintain an exhibition—and quite a bit.

I have also become more forgiving of early closing hours at museums. Before, I always thought it odd that the Natural History Museum in downtown Houston closes at six o'clock in the evening, but now I recognize how costly it is to staff a museum—especially late into the evening.

Museums—both large and small—rely on monetary gifts to function. Museums like the Texas Memorial, however, are trapped in a repeating cycle; they are too small to get the word out, and in turn receive few donations. Repeat.

The Texas Memorial Museum does not bring in much money—barely enough to function, let alone be an asset for the state. The museum itself is very small and hides nestled amongst other campus buildings; students who walk past it every day hardly know it exists.

While my perspective of museums has evolved, my reverence for them remains largely unchanged. The reason why I hold museums in high regard, however, has changed.

I used to admire museums for their engaging and didactic exhibitions. After studying museums in a larger context, however, what captivates me now is the immensity of work involved in creating a successful museum.

Designers, collectors, and curators all work together for one end product: the exhibition.

Part 6

The Activist

Chapter 18

And Then, the Phone Rang...

"Throughout the past three years, I have realized how important our work is [as museum professionals], not only for the objects themselves but for our communities and generations to come."

—HALLIE WINTER, CURATOR AT THE OSAGE NATION MUSEUM

The phone rang.

It was the Peruvian Consulate.

"We need your help."

***

Dirk Van Tuerenhout has been the curator of anthropology at the Houston Museum of Natural Science (HMNS) for over twenty years. Tuerenhout was born and raised across the pond in Belgium but moved to the United States to be closer to his field of interest: archaeology of the Americas.

Tuerenhout works at my favorite museum and in my field of study—he was, of course, among the first museum professionals I interviewed.

We set a date and time and agreed to meet at his office. He emailed me a map with directions to his office.

I don't need a map. I know the way to the HMNS like I know the back of my hand!

The address he sent me, however, didn't quite match up. It took me to a small, mid century building just minutes away from the museum campus. My destination was unlabeled on Google Maps, not to mention gated.

Tuerenhout, as I learned that day, works in the same building as the collections vault for the museum—among the most secretive locations in Houston.

***

"We have this altar piece—more than five-hundred-years old—laden with gold. It was stolen from a chapel in the Andes Mountains during a colonial raid. We finally discovered it in the home of a private collector. We need your help returning home to Peru."

Just days later, Tuerenhout and a colleague found themselves at the headquarters of U.S. Immigration and Customs Enforcement in Dallas, Texas.

"It was near the airport...but it wasn't Dallas/Fort Worth International," remembered Dirk.

"We're here to see Agent Johnson," Dirk said into the intercom.

A deep, imposing buzz sounded as the gates drifted open.

A member of the Peruvian consulate attended their meeting with the agent to discuss arrangements for returning the sacred artifact.

The agent told them the altar piece could be shipped on a diplomatic flight used to deliver supplies to embassies: things like printers, computers, and Xerox machines.

They carefully packed the altar into a massive crate and departed for Lima, Peru, where the U.S. ambassador had acquired funds to transport the altar back to the Andes Mountains—ensuring a safe turn to its original chapel.

Tuerenhout told me about another time his phone rang—this time, the Texas Department of Tourism was calling. A more ordinary caller, except the department usually calls the marketing, public relations, or visitor services divisions.

"Do you have an anthropology exhibit hall?"

"Yes," he replied.

"How many people visit the museum every year?"

"About two million. Though that could be better answered by the marketing department. What's this about?"

"There is the possibility of an exhibition traveling to the United States... from Ethiopia." A pregnant pause emitted from the other end of the line. "It involves Lucy."

For those unacquainted with paleoanthropology—the study of prehistoric human development—you might not have heard of Lucy before. She is the most famous paleoanthropological specimen discovered to date. Lucy's remains were discovered in 1974 by paleoanthropologist Donald Johanson in Ethiopia—while he was listening to "Lucy in the Sky with Diamonds."

What makes Lucy so special? First, she is one of the oldest fossils with evidence of bipedalism—the ability to habitually walk on two legs—in early humans. At the time, Lucy had never been on display outside of Ethiopia and was hardly ever displayed within Ethiopia.

Many in the United States initially rejected the idea of displaying Lucy; the Smithsonian turned down the opportunity on the principle that "Lucy should never leave Ethiopia." Presented with the opportunity to debut what would become a traveling exhibit, Tueren-hout believed the museum could do right by Ethiopia—who initiated the exhibition to raise awareness about Ethiopian history and culture.

After an agreement between the museum and the con-sulate, many trips to Ethiopia, and months of prepara-tion for the exhibit, Lucy was ready to be shipped across the Atlantic—with her own passport to boot.

Tuerenhout flew to Ethiopia to assist in the travel arrangements.

"She was treated with the utmost care," he emphasized. Only one representative from Ethiopia handled her bones through the entire process—weighing, wrapping, shipping, traveling, arrival, unpacking, weighing again, and displaying.

She arrived in New York early in the morning under the watchful gaze of the press.

In an attempt to undermine the exhibition, a reporter leaked to the press that Lucy was bound for New York—bad practice, since publicizing this fact puts the precious cargo at risk. Fortunately, though, Lucy arrived without a hitch and made her connecting flight to arrive safely in Houston.

After a successful run in Houston, five years traveling through the United States, and careful scanning at the University of Texas at Austin, it was time for Lucy to return home. Tuerenhout, along with Ethiopian diplomats and Lucy's original fossil-handler, accompanied her home.

Dirk recalls breathing a sigh of relief as soon as they landed—mission complete.

Strangely, though, the plane didn't pull right into the gate. It continued around the terminal until it halted in the middle of the tarmac. The seatbelt sign turned off and passengers began to unbuckle, but flight attendants asked that they remain seated to allow Lucy and her associates to disembark.

"I had no idea what was going on," Dirk explained.

As they filed out of the airplane, they were greeted with a fanfare of instruments, reporters, and cameras: Lucy's home!

***

"Never a dull moment." - Dirk Van Tuerenhout

Museum jobs are not boring. "Every day is different" Tuerenhout says, and his job is uniquely exciting. He's practically Indiana Jones.

Tuerenhout's adventures are just the tip of the iceberg in our exploration of issues related to provenance, display rights, and stolen artifacts.

Chapter 19

Righting Wrongs

"I believe in museums. I believe they have the power to change lives, inspire movements, and challenge authority."

—CINNAMON CATLIN-LEGUTKO, PRESIDENT
AND CEO OF THE ABBE MUSEUM

I had been looking forward to this trip for months.

In the summer of 2018, my brother and I flew to London to see the city, travel around the United Kingdom, and stay with my mother while she was there on business.

We went to at least two museums a day for two weeks straight.

We saved the best of all—the British Museum—for a weekend when our mom could join us. The British Museum houses the largest, most comprehensive display of human culture in the world. The museum is an absolute playground for a budding anthropologist like me.

I was so excited as we waited in line to enter the museum. I could barely hold it together. Ask my mom—she will tell you how her adult daughter was as antsy as a four-year-old. Other tourists in line were picking up on my energy—and definitely staring a little.

I was absolutely awestruck walking through those glass doors. I was like a kid in a candy store—my body could not take me to each artifact and gallery hall fast enough. I didn't have nearly enough time in the day to sit and meditate with hundreds of iconic objects.

The more I saw and read, however, the more this sense of awe began to diminish. I pondered the acquisition of the objects.

Many of the artifacts in the British Museum did not come from anywhere near the British Isles.

How did the British Museum come across so many wonderful objects? I could hardly believe countries were willing to part with these iconic, sacred artifacts.

Did they give them up willingly? Were they stolen? Were they spoils of war?

Do nations want their artifacts back?

***

The British Museum, main corridor

Established in 1753, the British Museum was the first public, national museum in the world.[1] What began as a collection of contemporary artifacts from across the globe is now a history museum—a monument to the past.

---

1   "History of the British Museum." The British Museum. Accessed September 14, 2019.

According to Patricia Galloway, professor in digital archiving at the University of Texas at Austin, an institution—in order to be considered a history museum—must celebrate something, must display a collective identity.

Especially in its early years, the British Museum celebrated the British Empire and the far lands to which it extended at the height of its reign. From the riverbeds of Southeast Asia to the deserts of Africa, the monarchy sent scholars all over the world to retrieve and study artifacts both ancient and modern. If a scholar deemed an object valuable, it would be taken back to London—often without the knowledge of local peoples and many times by force.

In some cases, the British Museum can be forgiven because many of these objects were stolen before ethical rules were established for anthropologists and archaeologists. Only in the latter half of the nineteenth century did anthropology and archaeology even become regulated professions.

Before then, no one needed a permit to open a dig site, and excavators often failed to keep effective records of the dig and items discovered during it. Scholars and looters alike lived by the rule of finders keepers.

Over two centuries later, many of these stolen artifacts still remain in the British Museum. The Rosetta Stone, the Elgin Marbles, the Benin Bronzes, and a statue from Easter Island all belong to this list of stolen items. These artifacts—and many others—do not represent British culture or identity and do not come from British soil. Instead, they represent a time of imperialism and colonial pillaging.

On the other hand, the British Museum is a brilliant and beautiful space to observe these artifacts—to see hundreds of global cultures come together in a single location. The British Museum provides an amazing opportunity, since it's nearly impossible for one person to travel the world in a lifetime.

At what cost, though? Now liberated from British rule, many nations have made efforts to request the return of such artifacts.

Repatriation (n.) is the process of returning an asset, an item of symbolic value, or a person to its owner or place of origin.[2]

Some museums own things, and some loan things, but museums should not own stolen items in the twenty-first century.

"Decolonizing the museum" has become something of an industry buzz-phrase. Dozens of museums, like the British Museum, have a history of acquiring items through colonialist empires. In the last decade, nations and peoples have begun to request that museums return those stolen treasures, and rightfully so.

Cinnamon Catlin-Legutko, president and CEO of the Abbe Museum in Bar Harbor, Maine, believes in the decolonization of museums. Catlin-Legutko is a passionate advocate for the intersection of museums with social justice and activism. She believes that—at a minimum—decolonization means "to share authority and governance for the interpretation and representation of native people."[3] American museums, specifically, house

---

2   *Merriam Webster Dictionary*, s.v. "repatriation," accessed October 25, 2019.

3   Catlin-Legutko, Cinnamon. YouTube. "We Must Decolonize Our Museums | Cinnamon Catlin-Legutko | TEDxDirigo." Filmed December 2016 in Maine, USA. Tedx Talks, 9:23.

a great deal of stolen artifacts from Native American peoples due to a long and troubled colonial history.

Amy Lonetree, a Ho-Chunk scholar, writes that "[m]useums can be painful institutions for native people as they are intimately tied to the colonization process."[4]

Across the pond in Britain, the case of the Elgin Marbles is a prominent example of a call for—and subsequent denial of—repatriation.

The Acropolis in Athens is a monumental complex from ancient Greece and a UNESCO World Heritage Site. The Parthenon, which rests atop the Acropolis, is an iconic symbol of ancient Greek culture.

At the beginning of the nineteenth century, Thomas Bruce, seventh earl of Elgin, was the British ambassador to the Ottoman Empire, to which Greece belonged at the time.

Bruce invited several skilled artists to make drawings of ancient monuments in Athens. He claimed he received a royal decree from the Ottoman Empire authorizing

---

4   Ibid.

him to take casts of the sculptures, fix the scaffolding around the Parthenon—and take any items of interest.

The edict from the Ottomans was admittedly ambiguous—Lord Elgin, however, believed it gave him carte blanche to take absolutely anything he might want.

Bruce and his men took several slabs of sculpted marble from the Parthenon, along with several sculptures and crates filled with other antiquities. They took several-thousand pounds of marble, well over two-thousand-years old at the time.

Bruce then sold the Elgin Marbles to Britain for thirty-five thousand pounds in 1816. They were placed in the British Museum, where they remain today.

Nassos Papalexandrou, professor of art history at the University of Texas at Austin, explained that Greece recently requested the marbles be returned to the Acropolis Museum. The British Museum denied that request, claiming the museum did not have adequate conditions to house the artifacts.

In response, Greece built a new, state-of-the-art Acropolis Museum—complete with space left specifically for the missing marbles. Even so, the British Museum, again, denied their request.

The original acquisition of the Elgin Marbles by the British was through looting in the infancy of proper archaeological ethics. They may have been stolen during a time of political unrest in Greece, but this cannot justify their continued stay in Britain. Now, more than ever—after millions spent to meet British demands—Greece deserves to have their artifacts returned.

Today, museums like the British Museum are pondering this issue of returning artifacts. If they return a handful of artifacts to their rightful owner, how many more will need to be returned?

If the British Museum returns the Elgin Marbles, they will lose an entire gallery of artifacts. The museum has also received calls to repatriate other artifacts, like the Benin Bronzes and a moai—a sort of monolithic figure— from Easter Island. Many objects are requested for cultural reasons in addition to issues of ownership. Laura Tarita Alarcón Rapu, governor of Easter Island, recently begged the British Museum to return the moai home due to its great spiritual value for the Rapa Nui people.

"You have our soul."

—LAURA TARITA ALARCÓN RAPU,
GOVERNOR OF EASTER ISLAND[5]

Hartwig Fischer, director of the British Museum, argues, "The collections have to be preserved as a whole."[6] The British Museum could certainly face reduced attendance if it chooses to return some of these iconic artifacts.

Who decides the protocol for the return of artifacts? What sort of exceptions are there, if any? Who decides what qualifies as 'adequate infrastructure' for the hosting of artifacts?

Museum professionals are currently attempting to answer these questions on a case by case basis.

Thousands of artifacts are displayed across the globe in countries they do not call home.

90 to 95 percent of sub-Saharan cultural

5   "Easter Island Governor Begs British Museum to Return Moai: 'You Have Our Soul'." The Guardian. Agence France-Presse, November 20, 2018.

6   Nayeri, Farah. "Return of African Artifacts Sets a Tricky Precedent for Europe's Museums." The New York Times, November 27, 2018.

artifacts on display are housed outside Africa.[7]

Ugochukwu-Smooth C. Nzewi, curator of painting and sculpture at the Museum of Modern Art in New York, envisions an industry where national ministries of culture, like UNESCO, set ethical frameworks to promote and supervise the repatriation of displaced artifacts.[8] The United Nations is equipped with the political power to take on such an endeavor.

Until such a program is implemented, museums are handling repatriation efforts on a museum-by-museum basis. The British Museum, for instance, is stuck in the past—but dozens of museums are making a conscious effort to right historic wrongs.

The Quai Branly Museum in Paris recently returned twenty-six cultural items looted by French-colonial forces to Benin.[9]

---

7   Jacobs, Emma. "Across Europe, Museums Rethink What to Do with Their African Art Collections." NPR, August 12, 2019.

8   Scher, Robin. "Better Safe Than Sorry: American Museums Take Measures Mindful of Repatriation of African Art -." ARTnews, June 11, 2019.

9   Jacobs, Emma. "Across Europe, Museums Rethink What to Do with Their African Art Collections." NPR, August 12, 2019.

The National Museum of the American Indian in Washington, DC, hosts a Repatriation Office with museum professionals dedicated to the systematic return of cultural items.

The Fowler Museum in Los Angeles, California, is "focusing internal efforts to establish guidelines for what they hold in their collections" based on where and how these artifacts were acquired by the museum.[10] Much of the museum's collection displays art and material culture from Africa, Asia, the Pacific, and the Americas—cultural items from thousands of miles away. The Fowler Museum recently stated that Native American representatives may submit a written request for an item in the collection.[11] The Native American Graves Protection and Repatriation Act (NAGPRA), which was ratified in 1990, has also provided guidance in this process of repatriation.

NAGPRA was enacted to address the rights of Native American and Native Hawaiian tribes, as well as their descendants, to certain cultural items—including human remains, funerary and sacred objects, and objects of

10   Scher, Robin. "Better Safe Than Sorry: American Museums Take Measures Mindful of Repatriation of African Art -." ARTnews, June 11, 2019.

11   National Park Service. "Notice of Intent To Repatriate Cultural Items: Fowler Museum at the University of California Los Angeles, Los Angeles, CA." Federal Register, October 19, 2018.

cultural patrimony. This legislation enforces that museums work together with native peoples to repatriate wrongfully-stolen items. NAGPRA also authorizes the secretary of the interior to administer grants to aid museums in complying with the statute.[12]

To help encourage repatriation globally, Nzewi suggests "a prospective framework whereby Western institutions pay royalty fees—which could be drawn from entrance fees and image-usage fees—to the rightful owners of stolen artworks in their collections."[13]

It's difficult to put a price on heritage. These artifacts are priceless to the communities to which they rightfully belong, but paying nations is a small offering to correct a massive cultural loss. The idea of reparations for historic wrongs is not novel, however.

---

12 Ellis, Linda. *Archaeological Method and Theory: An Encyclopedia*. New York: Garland Publishing, Inc., 2000.

13 Scher, Robin. "Better Safe Than Sorry: American Museums Take Measures Mindful of Repatriation of African Art -." ARTnews, June 11, 2019.

Reparation (n.) is the making of amends for a wrong one has done, by paying money to or otherwise helping those who have been wronged.[14]
For decades, policymakers and activists have studied the possibility of reparations to descendants of African American slaves in the United States, but no national legislation has been enacted. Small pay-out solutions, however, only fosters short-term thinking.

Elizabeth Merritt, founding director of the Center for the Future of Museums, says, "Money can't magically level the playing field" in issues of racial inequality.[15]

Nominal distribution of wealth would do little to solve structural inequalities, especially in the United States.

More has to be done to repay the collective cultural debt. The institutional system in America is rigged against nearly every minority in this country. Wouldn't it be more powerful to foster equal opportunity and support long-term equality rather than dole out payment to a select few?

---

14 *Merriam Webster Dictionary*, s.v. "reparations," accessed October 25, 2019.
15 Merritt, Elizabeth. "Building an Equitable Future: Museums and Reparations." American Alliance of Museums, June 19, 2019.

Museums have the power to aid in the resolution of inequality.

Merritt says museums have the opportunity to spread economic wealth separate from the government—without spending much money at all.[16]

Merritt advises museums to spread operational wealth by diversifying their staff, as well as their board of directors. This helps diversify the constituency of the museum and provides better representation of the community which the museum serves.[17]

46 percent of museum boards are entirely white.[18]

The American Alliance of Museums recently sponsored a four-million-dollar initiative to diversify museum boards across the nation.[19]

---

16 Ibid.

17 Ibid.

18 *Museum Board Leadership 2017: A National Report*, commissioned by the American Alliance of Museums and conducted by Board Source, 2017.

19 "51 Museums Selected for Board Diversity and Inclusion Program as Part of $4 Million National Initiative." American Alliance of Museums, July 23, 2019.

According to Merritt, diversifying operations creates access to intangible assets like "social connections, access to capital, knowledge, education and political power."[20]

> *"The beautiful thing is, unlike money, intangible assets like power, authority, and social networks can grow when they are shared."*
>
> —ELIZABETH MERRITT[21]

Merritt also suggests impact investing—investing the museum's endowments in programs that create positive societal or environmental change. Merritt says impact investing is hardly new—the 250-billion-dollar market is equipped with a variety of proven financial security measures.[22] Museums have the chance to help break the cycle and secure more capital for the institution in the process.

This extra capital could then be used toward reparation efforts. Museums can use extra capital to hire cultural advisers to develop new exhibits and programs that

---

20 Merritt, Elizabeth. "Building an Equitable Future: Museums and Reparations." American Alliance of Museums, June 19, 2019.

21 Ibid.

22 Ibid.

empower individuals within the community. Viewing an exhibit that speaks to you is an immensely powerful experience.

Museums have the power to influence culture and society as a trusted source of information. That power should be used for good.

* * *

It takes a village of advocates to promote any successful endeavor.

If you are a museum professional, you can attend Museums Advocacy Day in Washington, DC, to inform legislators about museums and the positive change which they bring to the table.

If you advocate for the decolonization of museums, write to the United Nations about imperialist museums wrongfully withholding artifacts from their rightful owners.

If you are a museum administrator, advocate the importance of diversifying your board of directors within your community.

If you are a curator, you have the unique creative freedom to generate more inclusive content in exhibition spaces—content that can have a positive impact beyond the halls.

Something can always be done, and museums have the power to do it.

"One of the great strengths of our sector is our organizations don't have to wait for political consensus to act. We can, instead, lead the way, using all the resources entrusted to us to build a better, more just, and equitable future."

—ELIZABETH MERRITT[23]

---

23   Ibid.

Chapter 20

The Keys to Museum Success

"*Never doubt that a small group of thoughtful, committed citizens can change the world; indeed, it is the only thing that ever has.*"

—MARGARET MEAD, AMERICAN ANTHROPOLOGIST

How do you measure a museum's success?

By the size of its collection? The size of its endowment? How many visitors grace the halls each year?

How can a museum be more successful? What is the secret sauce?

Look no further—I am about to reveal the keys to museum success. Not many know this to be possible and fewer try it, but the results are surely rewarding.

A successful museum in the twenty-first century is much more than money, accreditation, or acclaim.

A successful museum in the twenty-first century is—and should strive to be—relevant, inclusive, and modern.

This goal is easier said than done, of course. Perhaps no one museum perfectly embodies these characteristics just yet, but a handful are making great strides toward achieving them.

Relevance

What does it mean for a museum to be relevant?

In the process of conducting interviews for this book, every industry professional with whom I spoke said they wanted their museum to be relevant.

Museums, as an entire industry, are completely relevant—essential to the documentation and preservation of human culture, an ever-present part of our daily lives.

On a museum-by-museum basis, however, achieving relevance means garnering more attention, and therefore more visibility in the public eye and more daily visitors.

How do you achieve this coveted relevance? What's the magic formula?

The answer is actually very simple.

Relevant (adj.)—appropriate to the current time, period, or circumstances; of contemporary interest.[1]
If a social media influencer seeks to gain more followers, they participate in discussions and post about topics of contemporary interest. If a museum seeks to gain more visitors, it ought to do the same.

Media influencers who address current events get the most exposure. After all—who would watch the news two weeks later?

History is vital to understanding the present and the future, but a relevant museum looks to the present to help people understand the past. Visitors look to museums to provide this function.

A successful museum of the twenty-first century engages in discussions that are current and does not shy away from complex topics—from immigration to

---

1   *Merriam Webster Dictionary*, s.v. "relevant," accessed October 25, 2019.

mental illness, from renewable resources to the contamination of our oceans. People are drawn to these topics because they affect their daily lives. People love to see their perspectives and concerns echoed in the real world, and they are endlessly curious about the ultimate outcome.

Contemporary art museums often succeed in achieving relevance by displaying art that is reflective of the times because it was made so recently.

Relevant museums are not stuck in the past, not frozen in time. They continue evolving with their constituency and community.

Community involvement and engagement is where the museum can shine.

Inclusivity

A successful museum engages with its community and seeks to create a welcoming, encouraging environment.

Inclusivity is an ethical obligation, but practicing inclusivity will also help museums succeed. Positive press will undoubtedly attract more visitors and therefore more donors.

For a museum, being inclusive means being mindful of the needs of its constituency—current visitors as well as people who have not yet visited—and addressing those needs. Inclusivity can mean confronting a difficult question: why do some people choose not to visit? Museums should make a conscious effort to address that question and affect change in response.

Why do people choose not to visit museums?

Colleen Dilenschneider, expert in data analytics and museum marketing, says the price of admission is not to blame.[2] Other barriers are far more prominent: preferring alternative activities, feeling unwelcome, and negative previous experiences exceed cost concerns by far.

"Being free is not the same as being welcoming."

—COLLEEN DILENSCHNEIDER, CHIEF
MARKET ENGAGEMENT OFFICER AT IMPACTS
RESEARCH & DEVELOPMENT[3]

Friends often tell me museums are uninteresting. Interest comes from a connection or a passion, and non-vis-

---

2   Dilenschneider, Colleen. "They're Just Not That Into You: What Cultural Organizations Need to Know About Non-Visitors (DATA)." Colleen Dilenschneider, February 6, 2019.

3   Ibid.

itors are not connecting. People are more likely to go places where their interests, lifestyle, and identity are represented.

If you're a scientist or engineer, a museum of science and technology might be your favorite. If you loved to paint as a child, art museums might be wonderful places of solitude. If you love to read, historical museums might take you to places that let your imagination bloom.

How do museums help visitors connect? By being more inclusive—by channeling the interests and identities of their community and representing a wider audience.

We can look to the past—as far back as 1851—for examples of inclusivity in museum design. The Crystal Palace in Hyde Park, London, housed the Great Exhibition of 1851. It was nearly one-million square feet, made entirely of wall-to-wall glass. All exhibits could be seen by all people, and all people could be seen observing the exhibits. A museum made entirely of glass is about as transparent as it gets.

Inclusivity and accessibility go hand-in-hand—accessibility in transparency and view, accessibility in transportation and ease of access, and accessibility for disabled persons. Accessibility is design-driven.

More accessibility means more visitors. If people can see the museum, they are more likely to visit. The biggest and most popular museums are located in large cities with public transportation.

Some museums are going to great lengths to increase accessibility beyond what is required by law.

In 2010, about 56.7 million people, or 18.7 percent of the population, had some level of disability, according to the United States Census Bureau.[4]

"Museum designers have used a great deal of imagination, much more than is required by law, and do remarkable things," says Lex Frieden, executive director of the National Council on Disability.[5]

The Wellcome Collection in London strives to implement design features that aid disabled persons. The museum has painted displays to make them more accessible to the visually impaired, as well as set observation benches off-center to allow for wheelchair accessibility. These design elements are so beautifully subtle that

---

4   Mohn, Tanya. "Welcoming Art Lovers With Disabilities." The New York Times, October 25, 2013.

5   Ibid.

Clare Barlow, a curator at the museum, says, "If you don't need them, you might not notice them."[6]

"Accessibility is not ugly, or cluttered or distracting. Accessibility belongs in art and everywhere."

—CIARA O'CONNOR, A WHEELCHAIR USER, ON ISSUES OF ACCESSIBILITY AT THE TATE MODERN.[7]

The Smithsonian Institute has an entire program department devoted to accessibility. Led by Beth Ziebarth, director of the program, they invited visitors to record audio descriptions of art and artifacts in the collection.[8] The Smithsonian American Art Museum also offers special tours for blind and visually impaired visitors.[9]

The Whitney in New York City publishes video tours of the museum using American Sign Language and English captions. The Art Institute of Chicago even has plans

---

6   Marshall, Alex. "Is This the World's Most Accessible Museum?" The New York Times, September 6, 2019.

7   Ibid.

8   Mohn, Tanya. "Welcoming Art Lovers With Disabilities." The New York Times, October 25, 2013.

9   Stamberg, Susan. "Blind Art Lovers Make The Most Of Museum Visits With 'InSight' Tours." NPR, January 5, 2017.

to reproduce three-dimensional prints of artworks for visitors to touch.[10]

These museums utilize technology in creating accessible designs; most importantly, they consult differently-abled people when creating these features.

"If you've not got people who experience these issues in an organization, mistakes will be made," says Tony Heaton, a sculptor and wheelchair user.[11]

Having individuals actively participate in making change is itself an opportunity for inclusivity, as important as the implementation of new features. To further the goals of inclusivity, the American Alliance of Museums recently launched a three-year initiative called Facing Change: Museum Board Diversity and Inclusion. This initiative "will provide the framework, training, and resources for museum boards to build diverse and inclusive cultures within their organizations that better reflect and serve their communities."[12]

---

10 Mohn, Tanya. "Welcoming Art Lovers With Disabilities." The New York Times, October 25, 2013.

11 Marshall, Alex. "Is This the World's Most Accessible Museum?" The New York Times, September 6, 2019.

12 "Professional Development Through AAM Peer Review." *Museum Magazine*, Sept-Oct 2019.

Museums, like most nonprofits, typically have a board of directors that serves to advise the museum on major decisions. Diversifying boards will diversify museum events and visitors alike—making the museum more open and inviting to all. We live in a time where structural inequalities regarding race, gender, age, and ability cannot simply be ignored. Initiatives like Facing Change are essential to solving inequalities in a way that fosters lasting change.

Mary-Frances Winters, a passionate advocate for justice and equity, says the Golden Rule is no longer enough. "We need to advance to the Platinum Rule, which advises we treat people the way they want to be treated."[13]

Museum boards that keep things in the family and only consult familiar partners limit their own potential and are an obstacle to a more equitable future. Museums stand at the front lines in driving cultural change, and they need not wait on government bodies to make the change happen.

---

13 Winter, Mary Frances. "How Do We Make Change?" *Museum Magazine*, Sept-Oct 2019.

Modernity

A successful museum uses modern technology in exhibit design and social modernity to reach and impact wider audiences.

A modern museum is aware of the times and cultural climate—aware of itself, its community, and the changing fabric of our society. Museums cannot be content to exist as they always were—the world has changed since their opening day.

Eilean Hooper-Greenhill, professor emeritus of museum studies at the University of Leicester, describes contemporary museums as 'post-museums.' The museums of the late-nineteenth and early-twentieth centuries—what she calls 'modernist museums'—treated visitors as empty vessels to be filled with knowledge.[14] Modernist museums target the general public and treat everyone the same. Museums that function this way are not necessarily bad, but they do practice the bare minimum in outreach and inclusion.

Post-museums revolutionize the old way of museum pedagogy by doing away with the "expert to novice"

---

14 Hooper-Greenhill, Eilean. *Museums and the Interpretation of Visual Culture.* London: Routledge, 2008.

model.[15] Post-museums focus more on engaging the public in the material, accepting different levels of ability, and including various identities and narratives. In the post-museum, the audience becomes a source of validation.

In the post-museum, the audience becomes integral to the success of the exhibition—whereas in the modernist museum, success was determined by the subjective value of the collections.

Post-museums today are reorganizing museum culture to make visits into social experiences. As post-museums continue to incorporate outsider narratives, they invite visitors to engage with the material through features like performance and educational activities. Hooper-Greenhill says post-museums draw on constructivist learning theory, which conceives of "learning [as] both personal and social."[16]

Tony Bennett and his theory of the "exhibitionary complex" paved the way for the modern museum: no running, no photos, no shouting, no fun. But exhibition designers today—with the help of modern technology—are turning this set of rules on its head in the

---

15 Ibid.
16 Ibid.

post-modern museum. Post-museums want people to interact with objects.

A post-modern museum seeks to change. A post-modern museum is not content or complacent. A post-modern museum seeks to do better, to do right, and to do good for humankind.

***

My mom said to me once, "I don't like feeling stupid. I don't want to feel stupid when I go to a museum."

That's fair. Who would?

"Despite my reassurances to the contrary, they were worried they didn't have enough education about art history; that they would do something wrong; that they wouldn't understand or appreciate what they were viewing; that their personal beliefs would be challenged or offended; that they would feel inadequate and out of place. I began to realize that their reluctance to visit wasn't based on time, cost, or lack of interest, but rather deeply-held anxieties about who belongs in a museum."

—*ASHLEIGH HIBBINS FOR* MUSEUMPHILES[17]

17   Hibbins, Ashleigh. "San Antonio Museum of Art." The Museumphiles, January 23, 2016.

People assume knowledge will be expected of them at museums. The truth is, however, you go to a museum to learn. It is the job of the curator is to know everything about the exhibit, not yours.

Museums can relate current issues and knowledge to their exhibits to increase their relevance. The feeling of belonging or not belonging is the bigger issue, however—to solve this, look to relevance, inclusivity, and modernity.

Part 7

The Enthusiast

Chapter 21

A Museum is a Place That...

"The past causes the present, and so the future."

—*PETER STEARNS, FOUNDER OF THE JOURNAL OF SOCIAL HISTORY*

Through all the various rises and falls, people still love and believe in museums.

Museums are part of our everyday lives, and they are core to our identity as humans. Museums are special to people for a whole bunch of different reasons.

I asked everyday, extraordinary people to complete the sentence: A museum is a place that...

...represents what the public wants to see in the world.

—Jimmy Y.

...brings a sense of peace and brings pieces of the
past together.

—Marc W.

...connects us to the things that make us who we are.

—Jenny W.

...sparks joy.

—Eric K.

...is the closest thing to time travel.

—Isaiah C.

...takes me to a different place & time.

—Liza T.

...shows us our why. Why we exist; how we became;
who we are.

—Maddie B.

...inspires the soul!

—Sam F.

...is a window into what was once called the future.

—Mike H.

...a place that connects us to different places, and peoples, and times.

—Isaiah C.

...inspires through art and connection.

—Elisabeth F.

...teaches about the past and inspires the future.

—Laurel D.

...lets your mind take an adventure.

—Madeline M.

...lets you take a trip into another world and connects you with culture.

—Heather B.

...encourages curiosity for the world around us.

—Griffin R.

...is FUN!

—Taffy B.

...enlightens.

—Dawson F.

...starts a conversation!

—Aparna C.

...edifies your mind, body, and soul.

—Todd A.

...showcases the past, informs the present, and ignites
the future.

—David F.

...makes your mind wonder and wander.

—Michelle R.

...reminds us where we come from.

—Gleb T.

Not every museum is for everyone. Fortunately, there
are thousands of museums from which to choose, as
well as dozens of different types. There are so many
different reasons to love museums.

A museum also does so many things outside of teaching
and knowledge-building.

Memorializes the Past

The world commonly sees museums as places that memorialize the past. They are buildings—often big and old—filled with objects and artifacts of historical significance.

Museums are heritage sites—places with meaning and unifying identity.

Creates Buzz

Museums are always in the news.

A museum is a place where scientific discoveries are made and groundbreaking art goes on display.

Museums are a place to see and even to be seen. The annual gala for the Metropolitan Museum of Art is among the largest celebrity events of the year. More and more museums are utilizing social media to create photo opportunities for visitors to engage with the museum.

Encourages Creativity

A stigma exists that museums—especially art museums—are only for the elite and only display works by well-known artists. That is far from the truth, however.

Museums are places for artists and students alike. Art museums are places for artists to visit and learn from their predecessors—as they have done for centuries. Nineteenth-century painter Édouard Manet, for instance, would regularly visit the Louvre to mimic the masters.

Even in natural history museums, you will find the occasional artist sketching in the galleries.

"This is a space that encourages creativity," remarks John Maisano of the Texas Memorial Museum at the University of Texas at Austin.

"This is a place of inspiration. It's a place of learning. It's a place where you can just come and wander," Maisano adds.

Provides Relief

You can peacefully wander for hours inside a museum, and you can do many things to put your soul at ease— from prayer and worship to meditation and yoga.

Rothko Chapel, part of the Menil Collection in Houston, Texas, is quite literally a sanctuary of art, featuring works by American painter Mark Rothko.

The Natural History Museum in London regularly offers yoga in the grand hall.

The Isabella Stewart Gardner Museum in Boston is part museum and part lush oasis.

Builds Community

Post-museums are implementing new methods of community engagement. Museums are no longer just homes for knowledge. They are community centers with programs ranging from summer camps and art classes to cocktail hours and slumber parties.

The Museum of Fine Arts in Houston hosts a night for college students, complete with free admission and food trucks.

The Museum of Contemporary Art in Denver invites local teens to perform at an open mic night.

For its 'Night at the Museum' event, the Houston Museum of Natural Science stays open all night long—featuring flashlight tours and midnight snacks.

Museums strengthen bonds within communities and are safe spaces for social, cultural, and educational enrichment—which does nothing but good in the world.

Inspires the Future

What's in store for the future of museums? What's changing? What do we have to look forward to?

For one, more and more collections are going digital. Collection managers work for months to photograph, scan, and document items and materials to an online database. There, interested parties can learn about the artifacts without ever leaving the comfort of their own home. Museums are also beginning to curate collections that are exclusively online—a groundbreaking development for anyone facing travel restrictions.

Conservators are at the cutting edge of preservation methods—who knows what scientific implications these methods could have for other human problems.

Museums are also creating memorable, enriching experiences with the use of technology—virtual reality, augmented reality, holograms, sensors, touch screens, and more—that foster meaningful connections between humans and their surroundings.

Museums are preserving the past and propelling us into the future.

***

There will always be history to display. With every passing moment, people are always moving, creating, and discovering. Only we can decide what's worth remembering.

Since history is already being made, museums will always exist. We can't predict what form they will take in the future—but we can continue to enjoy them and support their evolution.

Chapter 22

A Little Purple Flier

"If I ever find myself with a few hours to spare, there's no place I'd rather be than a museum."

—AMRITA GURNEY, VICE PRESIDENT OF
MARKETING FOR CROWDRIFF[1]

In the beginning of 2017—halfway through my second year at the University of Texas—I changed my major from civil engineering to anthropology.

For me, it was a leap of faith—to leave behind a secure future to pursue a new passion. After all, what I liked the most about civil engineering was learning about humans interacting with their constructed environment, but my coursework was not offering me those lessons. The extraneous classes in my semester schedules were more exciting to me than those in my major.

---

1   Gurney, Amrita. "Attracting Visitors with User-Generated Content." American Alliance of Museums, June 24, 2019.

When I set out to change my major and leave engineering behind, I scoured the descriptions for every discipline and landed on anthropology. I'll admit—like many people—I had no idea what anthropology was at first. From my first lecture in linguistic anthropology, however, I've loved every minute of it. Biological, visual, acoustic, cultural, linguistic, archaeology—all endlessly fascinating to me.

Then, it got even better.

In the fall of 2017, I happened to visit an academic fair held outside the Flawn Academic Center at UT Austin. Looking from table to table, one flier in particular caught my eye: a purple one advertising museum studies. A sudden rush of endorphins and a feeling of pure, honest joy coursed through my veins. I applied for the program that eventually carried me all the way to an official certificate in museum studies.

***_

In addition to my intense enthusiasm for museums themselves, the study of museums has everything to do with anthropology. The course list for a museum studies certificate featured a series of anthropology courses, and my fascination with human behavior merged these two fields of study together for me. These thoughts launched me headfirst into the Bridging Disciplines Program for museum studies.

My first class, Museum Studies 101, was the inspiration for my project connecting the two disciplines. We took a class visit to Austin's Texas Memorial Museum and discussed science and natural history museums in context. Our thoughtful discussion about the evolution of natural history museums guided the topic of my research project: how have natural history museums evolved, and why does understanding their evolution matter? Over the course of my research, I learned a great deal about natural history museums and found a conclusion to my hypothesis by drawing on several other disciplines. I learned about how architecture affects the way people use space, and how technology drives visitation. I learned about the importance of image and marketing to the rates of visitation for a museum. I gained a new appreciation for the library system through many visits to libraries across campus. I even performed analysis on theme parks. I hadn't considered the idea that museums and theme parks are closely related until we studied it in one of my courses, Cultural Heritage on Display. At the end of this project I felt deeply invested in the program and was hungry for more.

The Texas Memorial Museum (TMM) served as my local example for research on natural history museums. My thoughtful conversations with the associate director of the museums led to another new experience—I became an external relations intern for the Texas Memorial Museum. I learned about the negligence of the state government in supporting an institution of immense historical significance and wanted to assistant by any means possible. I learned, too, that studying museology was more than just research—it's also about practice. Working at the Texas Memorial Museum taught me that running a museum and its exhibits takes cooperation between several different disciplines and professions.

From forming relationships with faculty and students to developing projects and partnerships for the museum, I saw a variety of perspectives. I also had the opportunity to collaborate with local artists and designers to create a new exhibit for TMM. In the long term, I feel this experience helped me to better understand the museum industry—and what it takes to keep the doors open every day.

"A good museum is an open museum."

A professor in a certificate class, Patricia Galloway, once told me, "A good museum is an open museum." Every week, we visited a museum, and every week, our professor would ask whether it was a good museum—which of course was a trick question. We learned a good museum is an open museum, and I take this perspective with me to every institution. My coursework gave me a newfound appreciation for the effort that goes into keeping a museum open—not to mention updated and changing.

Some of the most successful museums change and rotate their exhibits most often—bringing in new and exciting attractions regularly. I learned in my coursework that museums and theme parks are not entirely dissimilar; both live and thrive in the tourism industry and celebrate some cultural idea. All these experiences—my research, internship, and coursework—helped me to deepen my understanding and perspective. I now feel I have a richer appreciation for museums than ever before.

For museum enthusiasts and those curious about various human values—what and why certain exhibits are displayed—I would recommend books on museology, like this one. The discipline of museum studies goes far beyond museums alone and takes a wider anthropological perspective—one I think we don't consider all that often.

Each of my courses was intensified through collaboration with other experiences. I would not have started my research without the knowledge I gained from Museum Studies 101, I may not have found the appropriate conclusion to my research without Cultural Heritage on Display. I might not have found an internship at the Texas Memorial Museum without touring it in Museum Studies 101 or researching it for my first interdisciplinary experience. Each of these experiences built on one another and deepened my understanding my solidifying ideas I'd only considered in the past.

Let this be yet another lesson about the importance of context and collaboration between various disciplines. I found the context I craved through my experiences. As I reflect on my coursework, museum adventures, new colleagues, and even this book, I realize all these things were made possible by the path that began with a little, purple flier.

Acknowledgments

Thank you.

There are an endless number of people I have to thank for making this book possible. This is quite possibly one of the hardest things I have ever done, and I owe so much of my success to the aid of so many wonderful people. No one achieves anything alone, and that has certainly been clear from the beginning of this incredible journey.

I'd like to thank;

My parents — for being my superfans: in my pre-order campaign and in life.

My brother, Dawson Finklea — for thoughtful conversations that inspired many of my words, and for being one of the smartest and most articulate people I know.

My friends—for sitting with me through late nights at Austin's finest coffeehouses and tagging along with me on countless museum visits.

Carol Ansel—for being one of the first people to recognize my writing potential.

Kathleen Stewart—for teaching me to write without judgment.

Stephanie McKibben and Angela Ivey—for helping me find the core purpose of this book and leading me through the development of my manuscript.

Eric Koester—for so many things. Thank you for being the first to pre-order, for investing your time with me, for inviting me on this incredible journey, and for being my mentor.

Brian Bies—for putting up with all of the ups and downs of getting this book into the hands of millions.

Tom Schwenk—for being a huge supporter of the production of this book and for being everything I want to be when I grow up: a philanthropic spirit who always encourages and mentors the newest generation.

Thomas Hankey — for helping make a hardcover possible.

Karen Alberstadt—for supporting me in the pre-order campaign and in life. Always.

Billy Wood—for contributing immensely to the pre-order campaign and for the adventure of a lifetime. Vienna forever!

Jack Wyatt III—for being my number one fan and a champion for my education.

Lastly, I want to acknowledge anyone who has supported me throughout this process, anyone who has pre-ordered this book, and anyone who is buying it when it releases.

Thank you all so much for your endless support and encouragement. This book is a first step for me into a brighter future in this industry, and I very much look forward to what's next.

References

Chapter I

Duffer, Ellen. 2019. "Readers Still Prefer Physical Books". *Forbes. Com*. https://www.forbes.com/sites/ellenduffer/2019/05/28/readers-still-prefer-physical-books/#77fe13fo1fdf.

Chapter II

Dilenschneider, Colleen. 2019. "Admission Fees Aren't What Keep Millennials From Visiting Cultural Organizations (DATA) - Colleen Dilenschneider". *Colleen Dilenschneider*. https://www.colleendilen.com/2019/07/31/admission-fee-isnt-what-keeps-millennials-away-from-cultural-organizations-data/.

Gao, Rebecca. 2018. "We Asked Gen Z About Their Spending Habits". Vice. https://www.vice.com/en_us/article/d3kd7q/we-asked-gen-z-about-their-spending-habits.

Kondō, Marie. *Spark Joy: An Illustrated Master Class on the Art of Organizing and Tidying Up.* Ten Speed Press, 2016.

Museums as Economic Engines: A National Study, commissioned by the American Alliance of Museums and conducted by Oxford Economics, 2017.

Museums of The World 2017. 2017. 24th ed. Berlin: De Gruyter Saur.

Chapter 1

Chesser, Preston. 2019. "The Burning Of The Library Of Alexandria | Ehistory". *Ehistory.Osu.Edu.* https://ehistory.osu.edu/articles/burning-library-alexandria.

"Museum Definition - ICOM". 2019. *ICOM.* https://icom.museum/en/activities/standards-guidelines/museum-definition/.

Museums and Public Opinion: Summary of Findings from National Public Opinion Polling, commissioned by the American Alliance of Museums and conducted by Wilkening Consulting, 2018.

Ryan, Julia. 2013. "Study: Students Really Do Learn Stuff On Field Trips". The Atlantic. https://www.theatlantic.com/education/archive/2013/09/study-students-really-do-learn-stuff-on-field-trips/279720/.

Chapter 2

None

Chapter 3

"Chicago Museum Campus | Enjoy Illinois". 2019. *Enjoy Illinois*. https://www.enjoyillinois.com/explore/listing/chicago-museum-campus.

Contributor, Jessie. 2018. "The Louvre Museum: Facts, Paintings & Tickets". *Livescience.Com*. https://www.livescience.com/31935-louvre-museum.html.

Dilenschneider, Colleen. 2019. "Inactive Visitors Are Interested in Attending Cultural Organizations. Why Don't They? (DATA) - Colleen Dilenschneider". *Colleen Dilenschneider*. https://www.colleendilen.com/2019/01/30/inactive-visitors-are-interested-in-attending-cultural-organizations-why-dont-they-data.

"Family Guide". 2019. Dallas. Dallas Museum of Art. Dallas Museum of Art.

"Gallery Feet". 2007. Podcast. *Moment Of Science*. https://indianapublicmedia.org/amomentofscience/gallery-feet/.

"Park Güell - Regulation Conditions For Group Access | April 2013". 2019. Barcelona: Barcelona de Serveis Municipals. https://www.

barcelonaturisme.com/imgfiles/Professionals/Park-Güell_Condicions_Abril%202013-ang.pdf.

Chapter 4

Bennett, Tony. "The Exhibitionary Complex." In *Representing the Nation: A Reader*, edited by David Boswell and Jessica Evans, 333–358. London and New York: Routledge, 1999.

Gray, Nick. "How I learned to stop hating and love museums | Nick Gray | TEDxFoggyBottom." Filmed May 2015 in Washington, DC. TEDx Talks, 17:30. https://www.youtube.com/watch?v=6VW-PHKABRQA.

Kjartansson, Ragnar. "The Visitors," Video, 2012.

Chapter 5

Andi Stein, Beth Bingham Evans. 2009. *An Introduction to the Entertainment Industry*. New York: Peter Lang Publishing.

Fagan, Brian. 2018. *Little History of Archaeology*. New Haven and London: Yale University Press.

"Hidden Layers: Painting and Process in Europe, 1500–1800". 2018. Houston: Museum of Fine Arts Houston. https://www.mfah.org/exhibitions/hidden-layers-painting-process-europe-1500-1800

Oprea, John. "Geometry and the Foucault Pendulum." *The American Mathematical Monthly*102, no. 6 (1995): 515–22. https://doi.org/10.2307/2974765.

"The French National Museum of Natural History." Convention on Biological Diversity. Secretariat of the Convention on Biological Diversity, April 3, 2008. http://www.cbd.int/cooperation/mnhn.shtml.

Vincent H. Rash, Ring T. Cared. 2003. *Encyclopedia of Insects*. London: Elsevier.

Chapter 6

Cotton, Jess. "What Art Museums Should Be For." The Book of Life. The School of Life, August 24, 2016. https://www.theschooloflife.com/thebookoflife/utopian-art-museums/?utm_source=You%20Tube&utm_medium=You%20Tube%20-%20What%20Art%20Museum%20Are%20For%20-%20Video%20Description%20-%20TBOL%20Article&utm_campaign=You%20Tube%20-%20What%20Art%20Museum%20Are%20For%20-%20Video%20Description%20-%20TBOL%20Article.

Disturnell, John. *New York As It Was and As It Is*. New York, NY: D. Van Nostrand, 1876.

Martin, Jeff. "Go Forward Move Ahead". *Museum Confidential*. NPR, September 20, 2019. https://www.npr.org/podcasts/557204718/ museum-confidential.

Oliver, Bette Wyn. 2007. *From Royal to National: The Louvre Museum and the Bibliothèque Nationale*. Lanham: Lexington Books.

"The Acquisition of J.E. Gotzkowsky's Collection by Catherine II." 1764 The Acquisition of J.E. Gotzkowsky's Collection by Catherine II. Accessed November 8, 2019. https://www.hermitagemuseum.org/ wps/portal/hermitage/explore/history/historical-article/1750/ Empress Catherine II purchases Johann Ernest Gotzkowskis collection/!ut/p/z1/jZDdToQwEIVfpT6A6cDCLntZKxRYsOIv-9sYopEKzbEsoarJPLxpv1IjO3WS-mTnnYIFrLIx8oa2ctDWyn_sHsX7khKy9FYWcXV8AEFpUZ1dFnO6iAN9_APBLEcDiP_sLg-Fg-n__1YHbgjyUtWywGOXWn2jxZXHubEHAdH4ZROYfoPF-CjNgplGRqex6aTTjmU204ag-LRKDchZqfj3r66vXaosX2vmve-MZgPiq4RomyZAgjipSLm6pKH3HWAJOwfCthWNAu6z6A-fAs9oGCL8JU87vqE-DT2AhhuFwWx-LFHTWnrwBd6rNjw!!/ dz/d5/L2dBISEvZoFBIS9nQSEh/?lng=en.

The Editors of Encyclopaedia Britannica. "Pennsylvania Academy of the Fine Arts." Encyclopædia Britannica. Encyclopædia Britannica, Inc., September 27, 2006. https://www.britannica.com/ topic/Pennsylvania-Academy-of-the-Fine-Arts.

"The World's Oldest Museums." Museums of the World Museums. Semantika. Accessed November 8, 2019. https://museu.ms/highlight/details/105317/the-worlds-oldest-museums.

Watkins, Katie. "Inside Look: More Than 50 Rarely-Loaned Van Gogh Works On Display at The Museum of Fine Arts, Houston." Houston Public Media, March 18, 2019. https://www.houstonpublicmedia.org/articles/news/in-depth/2019/03/18/325542/inside-look-more-than-50-rarely-loaned-van-gogh-works-on-display-at-the-museum-of-fine-arts-houston/.

YouTube. "A World of Art: The Metropolitan Museum of Art." Great Museums, December 9, 2009. https://www.youtube.com/watch?v=PHrmoSlfLD0.

Chapter 7

Barto, Jillian. "The New House Museum: How the Development of Modern House Museums Are Changing the Philosophies and Standards of Interpretation and Preservation." 2012.

De Gorgas, Mónica Risnicoff. "Reality as Illusion, the Historic Houses That Become Museums." *Museum Studies: An Anthology of Contexts*, 2nd ed., Wiley-Blackwell (2012): 324–328.

Dichtl, John. "Most Trust Museums as Sources of Historical Information." AASLH, February 20, 2018. https://aaslh.org/most-trust-museums/.

Giovanni Pinna. "Introduction to Historic House Museums," Museum International 53 (2001): 4-9.

"Home Page." AASLH. Accessed 2018. https://aaslh.org/.

Lowenthal, David. "The Practice of Heritage." *The Heritage Crusade and the Spoils of History*, Free Press (1996): 148–172.

Chapter 8

Reid, Lauren. "The Secret Life of Objects: Strategies for Telling New Stories in Exhibitions." Allegra, September 16, 2018. https://t.co/9klrYFWoEe?ssr=true.

United States Mint. 2010. *United States Mint annual report.* Washington, D.C.: U.S. Mint. https://www.usmint.gov/wordpress/wp-content/uploads/2019/06/US-Mint-2010-Annual-Report.pdf.

Chapter 9

"Air-Conditioning System Caused Brazil Museum Fire, Say Police." The Japan Times, April 5, 2019. https://www.japantimes.co.jp/

news/2019/04/05/world/science-health-world/air-condition-
ing-system-caused-brazil-museum-fire-say-police/.

Chacoff, Alejandro. "Brazil Lost More Than the Past in the National
Museum Fire." The New Yorker. The New Yorker, September 16,
2018. https://www.newyorker.com/news/dispatch/brazil-lost-
more-than-the-past-in-the-national-museum-fire.

Garner, Katherine. "Robert Frost's Nothing Gold Can Stay: Poem
Meaning & Analysis." Study.com. Accessed September 8, 2019.
https://study.com/academy/lesson/robert-frosts-nothing-gold-
can-stay-poem-meaning-analysis.html.

Hogue, Adam. "Banksy Street Art: When Street Art Is in a Museum,
What's the Point?" Mic, May 13, 2013. https://www.mic.com/arti-
cles/41397/banksy-street-art-when-street-art-is-in-a-museum-
what-s-the-point.

Leasca, Stacey. "Officials Say These Two Things May Have Caused
Notre Dame Fire." Travel Leisure, June 28, 2019. https://www.
travelandleisure.com/travel-news/notre-dame-fire-cause.

Moody, Ellen. YouTube. "LIVE Q&A with MoMA Painting & Sculpture Conservators Ellen & Diana (March 14)." The Museum
of Modern Art, March 14, 2018. https://www.youtube.com/
watch?v=_QzzLGluPZ8

Temer, Michael. Twitter Post. September 3, 2018, 5:59 PM. https://
    twitter.com/MichelTemer/status/1036418286534238208

YouTube. "Makes a Difference (S2, E6) | AT THE MUSEUM." The
    Museum of Modern Art, October 18, 2019. https://www.youtube.
    com/watch?v=IpjTNdquCkg&list=PLfYVzkosNiGEgFGeTqyFNk-
    7g7o3rBrh37

Chapter 10

None

Chapter 11

Clifford, James. *The Predicament of Culture: Twentieth-century Ethnog-
    raphy, Literature, and Art.* Cambridge, MA: Harvard University
    Press, 2002.

Pogrebin, Robin. "Clean House to Survive? Museums Confront
    Their Crowded Basements." The New York Times, March 10,
    2019. https://www.nytimes.com/interactive/2019/03/10/arts/
    museum-art-quiz.html.

Stewart, Susan. *On Longing: Narratives of the Miniature, the Gigantic,
    the Souvenir, the Collection.* Durham and London: Duke University
    Press, 1993.

Sturken, Marita, and Lisa Cartwright. *Practices of Looking: An Intro-duction to Visual Culture*. New York: Oxford University Press, 2001.

Chapter 12
None

Chapter 13
"Gems and Minerals – Beauties and Building Blocks." Smithsonian National Museum of Natural History. Accessed November 8, 2019. https://naturalhistory.si.edu/education/teaching-resources/earth-science/gems-and-minerals-beauties-and-building-blocks.

Gopnik, Blake. "A Record Picasso And the Hype Price of Sta-tus Objects." The Washington Post. WP Company, May 7, 2004. https://www.washingtonpost.com/archive/life-style/2004/05/07/a-record-picasso-and-the-hype-price-of-sta-tus-objects/91826269-6a9e-42a4-91e8-3ec3aed10510/.

"Highest Insurance Valuation for a Painting." Guinness World Records. Accessed November 8, 2019. https://www.guinnessworldrecords.com/world-records/highest-insurance-valuation-for-a-painting.

Chapter 14

Beard, Mary. "Souvenirs of Culture: Deciphering (in) the Museum."
    Art History 15, no. 4 (December 1992): 505–32.

"History of the British Museum." The British Museum. Accessed
    September 14, 2019. https://www.britishmuseum.org/about_us/
    the_museums_story/general_history.aspx.

Chapter 15

"Museum Facts & Data." American Alliance of Museums, December
    11, 2018. https://www.aam-us.org/programs/about-museums/
    museum-facts-data/.

"The Business Model of the Nonprofit Museum." Sotheby's Institute
    of Art. Accessed September 28, 2019. https://www.sothebysin-
    stitute.com/news-and-events/news/the-business-model-of-the-
    nonprofit-museum/.

Chapter 16

"About." MICRO. Accessed October 22, 2019. https://micro.ooo/#about.

"About." Virmuze. Accessed October 22, 2019. https://virmuze.com/
    about/.

Isselhardt, Tiffany Rhoades. "Collecting Girlhood: Why the New Activist Museum Is Virtual." American Alliance of Museums, April 9, 2019. https://www.aam-us.org/2019/04/10/collecting-girlhood-why-the-new-activist-museum-is-virtual/.

Team, BoF. "Inside Valentino Garavani's Virtual Museum." The Business of Fashion, December 7, 2011. https://www.businessoffashion.com/articles/digital-scorecard/digital-scorecard-valentino-garavani-virtual-museum.

Chapter 17

Beard, Mary. "Souvenirs of Culture: Deciphering (in) the Museum." *Art History* 15, no. 4 (December 1992): 505–32.

Chapter 18

None

Chapter 19

"51 Museums Selected for Board Diversity and Inclusion Program as Part of $4 Million National Initiative." American Alliance of Museums, July 23, 2019. https://www.aam-us.org/2019/07/23/51-museums-selected-for-board-diversity-and-inclusion-program-as-part-of-4-million-national-initiative/.

Catlin-Legutko, Cinnamon. YouTube. "We Must Decolonize Our Museums | Cinnamon Catlin-Legutko | TEDxDirigo." Filmed December 2016 in Maine, USA. Tedx Talks, 9:23. https://www.youtube.com/watch?v=jyZAgG8***Xg

"Easter Island Governor Begs British Museum to Return Moai: 'You Have Our Soul'." The Guardian. Agence France-Presse, November 20, 2018. https://www.theguardian.com/world/2018/nov/20/easter-island-british-museum-return-moai-statue.

Ellis, Linda. *Archaeological Method and Theory: An Encyclopedia*. New York: Garland Publishing, Inc., 2000.

"History of the British Museum." The British Museum. Accessed September 14, 2019. https://www.britishmuseum.org/about_us/the_museums_story/general_history.aspx.

Jacobs, Emma. "Across Europe, Museums Rethink What to Do with Their African Art Collections." NPR, August 12, 2019. https://www.npr.org/2019/08/12/750549303/across-europe-museums-rethink-what-to-do-with-their-african-art-collections.

Merriam Webster Dictionary, s.v. "reparations," accessed October 25, 2019. https://www.merriam-webster.com/dictionary/reparations

Merriam Webster Dictionary, s.v. "repatriation," accessed October 25, 2019. https://www.merriam-webster.com/dictionary/repatriation

Merritt, Elizabeth. "Building an Equitable Future: Museums and Reparations." American Alliance of Museums, June 19, 2019. https://www.aam-us.org/2019/06/19/building-an-equitable-future-museums-and-reparations/.

Museum Board Leadership 2017: A National Report, commissioned by the American Alliance of Museums and conducted by Board Source, 2017.

National Park Service. "Notice of Intent To Repatriate Cultural Items: Fowler Museum at the University of California Los Angeles, Los Angeles, CA." Federal Register, October 19, 2018. https://www.federalregister.gov/documents/2018/10/19/2018-22792/notice-of-intent-to-repatriate-cultural-items-fowler-museum-at-the-university-of-california-los.

Nayeri, Farah. "Return of African Artifacts Sets a Tricky Precedent for Europe's Museums." The New York Times, November 27, 2018. https://www.nytimes.com/2018/11/27/arts/design/macron-report-restitution-precedent.html.

Scher, Robin. "Better Safe Than Sorry: American Museums Take Measures Mindful of Repatriation of African Art -." ARTnews, June 11, 2019. http://www.artnews.com/2019/06/11/african-art-repatriation-american-museums/.

Chapter 20

Dilenschneider, Colleen. "They're Just Not That Into You: What Cultural Organizations Need to Know About Non-Visitors (DATA)." Colleen Dilenschneider, February 6, 2019. https://www. colleendilen.com/2019/02/06/theyre-just-not-that-into-you-what-cultural-organizations-need-to-know-about-non-visitors-data/.

Hibbins, Ashleigh. "San Antonio Museum of Art." The Museum-philes, January 23, 2016. https://museumphiles.wordpress.com/tag/san-antonio-museum-of-art/.

Hooper-Greenhill, Eilean. *Museums and the Interpretation of Visual Culture.* London: Routledge, 2008.

Marshall, Alex. "Is This the World's Most Accessible Museum?" The New York Times, September 6, 2019. https://www.nytimes.com/2019/09/06/arts/design/disabled-access-wellcome-collection.html.

Merriam Webster Dictionary, s.v. "relevant," accessed October 25, 2019. https://www.merriam-webster.com/dictionary/relevant

Mohn, Tanya. "Welcoming Art Lovers With Disabilities." The New York Times, October 25, 2013. https://www.nytimes.com/2013/10/27/arts/artsspecial/welcoming-art-lovers-with-disabilities.html?action=click&module=RelatedLinks&pgtype=Article.

"Professional Development Through AAM Peer Review." *Museum Magazine*, Sept-Oct 2019.

Stamberg, Susan. "Blind Art Lovers Make The Most Of Museum Visits With 'InSight' Tours." NPR, January 5, 2017. https://www.npr.org/sections/health-shots/2017/01/05/505419694/blind-art-lovers-make-the-most-of-museum-visits-with-insight-tours.

Winter, Mary Frances. "How Do We Make Change?" *Museum Magazine*, Sept-Oct 2019.

Chapter 21

None

Chapter 22

Gurney, Amrita. "Attracting Visitors with User-Generated Content." American Alliance of Museums, June 24, 2019. https://www.aam-us.org/2019/06/24/attracting-visitors-with-user-generated-content/?fbclid=IwAR2RgRKUicR2oHLVshD4AIWwArdoh-Sc7ShmVy3T1tBq4w5DA-Z2dY96zDq4.